T0247735

Don't Forget to Live

THE FRANCE CHICAGO COLLECTION

*A series of books translated with the generous support of the
University of Chicago's France Chicago Center*

Don't Forget to Live

Goethe and the Tradition of
Spiritual Exercises

Pierre Hadot

Translated by Michael Chase

With a foreword by Arnold I. Davidson and Daniele Lorenzini

The University of Chicago Press
Chicago and London

The University of Chicago Press, Chicago 60637
The University of Chicago Press, Ltd., London
Published 2023
Printed in the United States of America

32 31 30 29 28 27 26 25 24 23   1 2 3 4 5

ISBN-13: 978-0-226-49716-7 (cloth)
ISBN-13: 978-0-226-49733-4 (e-book)
DOI: https://doi.org/10.7208/chicago/9780226497334.001.0001

N'oublie pas de vivre: Goethe et la tradition des exercices spirituels
© Editions Albin Michel—Paris 2008

Library of Congress Cataloging-in-Publication Data

Names: Hadot, Pierre, author. | Chase, Michael, 1959– translator.
Title: Don't forget to live : Goethe and the tradition of spiritual exercises /
    Pierre Hadot ; translated by Michael Chase.
Other titles: N'oublie pas de vivre. English (Chase) | Goethe and the
    tradition of spiritual exercises
Description: Chicago : The University of Chicago Press, 2023. |
    Includes bibliographical references and index.
Identifiers: LCCN 2022026307 | ISBN 9780226497167 (cloth) |
    ISBN 9780226497334 (ebook)
Subjects: LCSH: Goethe, Johann Wolfgang von, 1749–1832—Criticism and
    interpretation. | Goethe, Johann Wolfgang von, 1749–1832—Philosophy. |
    Philosophy, Modern—19th century.
Classification: LCC PT2193 .H2313 2023 | DDC 831/.6—dc23/eng/20220713
LC record available at https://lccn.loc.gov/2022026307

To my grandson Adrien Pagano.
As a token of gratitude
for all that he has brought to me.

Contents

Foreword

Don't Forget to Read

People do not know what it costs in time and effort to learn to read. I needed eighty years for this and I'm not even able to say if I have succeeded.[1]

Those who are familiar with Pierre Hadot's celebrated work on the history of Greco-Roman philosophy, and with some of his most famous books, such as *Philosophy as a Way of Life* or *What Is Ancient Philosophy?*,[2] will no doubt be surprised to discover that his last published monograph was devoted to a modern literary author—a poet, novelist, and playwright with scientific interests: Johann Wolfgang von Goethe.[3] The temptation will be great to glance at the title and back cover of this book, and to immediately and hastily conclude that the book must not be a philosophy book after all, but (at best) an exercise in literary criticism, of interest primarily to Goethe scholars.

This would be, of course, a serious mistake, albeit one that has its roots in a widespread conception that philosophers have of what counts and what doesn't count as philosophy, and of who is and who isn't a philosopher properly speaking. It has been, and still is, an occupational obsession for philosophers to trace the boundaries of their discipline and enforce them against any unwanted intrusion.

A real philosopher, we are told, must work on a set of well-defined (metaphysical, epistemological, ethical, political, or aesthetic) problems, and must elaborate responses to those problems that take the form of a systematic "doctrine," or at least of a coherent "theory" with explanatory and/or normative power. As Richard Rorty already remarked in 1976:

> Ever since philosophy became a self-conscious and professional-ized discipline, around the time of Kant, philosophers have enjoyed explaining how different their subject is from such merely "first-intentional" matters as science, art, and religion. Philosophers are forever claiming to have discovered methods which are presuppo-sitionless, or perfectly rigorous, or transcendental, or at any rate *purer* than those of non-philosophers. . . . Philosophers who betray this gnostic ideal (Kierkegaard and Dewey, for example) are often discovered not to have been "real philosophers."[4]

Institutional affiliation is now also systematically used as a distinctive mark of belonging: if you don't work in a university philosophy department, you surely aren't a real philosopher!

In *Don't Forget to Live*, Hadot defies these entrenched and preju-dicial narratives and problematizes the dogmatic aspect of these dis-ciplinary practices. By putting Goethe next to canonical figures in the history of philosophy such as Plato, Seneca, Epictetus, Marcus Aurelius, or Nietzsche, he questions the rigid idea that philosophers have of their own discipline, and their way of writing the history of phi-losophy itself. This, of course, should not entirely come as a surprise for the careful reader of Hadot: his redefinition of philosophy, not as a set of doctrines and theories, but as a practice of self-transformation and a way of life, entails the urgent task of redrawing the boundaries between philosophy and other disciplines. Even more radically, by characterizing philosophy's fundamental endeavor in terms of the elaboration and practice of a series of "spiritual exercises"—which, as he insists once more in the preface to this book, do *not* inevitably have any religious connotation, but are "acts of the intellect, or of the imagination, or of the will," by means of which "the individual tries to transform their way of seeing the world, in order to transform themselves"[5]—Hadot implicitly suggests that drawing those boundaries *in advance* will always lead us to exclude from the domain of philosophy figures and texts that are, in fact, fundamental to it.

One of Hadot's main goals is to get his readers to understand that operating with a preformed and fixed idea of who should count as a philosopher and who shouldn't will necessarily lead them to unduly limit their chances to read and experience a variety of ancient and modern texts as occasions to practice philosophy as an exercise of self-transformation, at one and the same time intellectual and ethical. This insight is crucial to understanding why Hadot treats Goethe as a philosopher *tout court*, attributing to his texts a philosophical relevance as significant as Epictetus's or Nietzsche's texts. In Hadot's view, Goethe is one of the most important modern thinkers to reactivate the ancient conception of philosophy as a way of life. As Hadot convincingly shows in this book, Goethe reflects upon and practices some of the very same spiritual exercises that also characterized ancient philosophy: the exercise of concentration on the present moment, the so-called "view from above," cosmic consciousness, and the "Yes" to life and the world in both their exhilarating and their terrifying aspects. Through these exercises, Goethe, as many others before him, attempts to detach himself from his particular and partial perspective, and to attain thereby universality and objectivity—at least as far as any human being can—and to conjoin the traditional *memento mori* (Don't forget that you will die) with the Spinozian *memento vivere* (Don't forget to live in the present), two philosophically intertwined experiences.

Hadot's conception of philosophy, characterized by the claim that philosophical discourse should ultimately be in the service of philosophical life, thus clearly opens up the possibility of recognizing the philosophical relevance and insight of works that are traditionally considered as belonging to disciplines different from philosophy:

poems, novels, plays, paintings and sculptures, pieces of music, movies—insofar as they can all (at least potentially) contribute to the transformation of ourselves and our lives. They merit being conceived of as domains that give rise to spiritual exercises analogous to those practiced by, for example, Marcus Aurelius or Epictetus.

In a general way we can say that art, poetry, literature, painting, or even music can be a spiritual exercise. The best example is the work of Proust, because his search for lost time is an itinerary of consciousness, which, thanks to the exercises of memory, rediscovers the sentiment of its spiritual permanence. This is very Bergsonian.[6]

The point here isn't to treat poems, paintings, or pieces of music as interesting examples to use in a philosophy book in order to better *illustrate* a theoretical argument, but to attribute to them the status of *philosophical contributions* in their own right. Of course, not every text, work of art, or piece of music can actually play this transformative role, but there is no reason to exclude any of them a priori—just because they don't belong to the preformed idea we have of philosophy. Moreover, not all texts belonging to the traditional philosophical canon also belong to the tradition or conception of philosophy as a way of life that Hadot uncovers and valorizes in his works. Yet the latter conception of philosophy can also be helpfully used to look at some texts in a different light, emphasizing aspects of them that would go unnoticed if all we cared about were abstract concepts and theories.

In short, Hadot urges us to rethink our idea of philosophy not in order to replace the traditional, dogmatic idea we have of philosophy with a different but equally dogmatic definition of it, but to allow us to see philosophical value in a variety of different forms of human creation—and perhaps to realize that, no matter our day job, we can aspire to and live a philosophical life, if only we make that existential choice.

Arnold I. Davidson and Daniele Lorenzini

Translator's Introduction

The present work is a translation of *N'oublie pas de vivre: Goethe et la tradition des exercices spirituels*, the last published monograph by Pierre Hadot, who died two years after its publication in 2008.

In many ways, it is one of Hadot's most personal works. As he looks back after eighty years of life, well aware of his approaching death, he turns to one of the guiding spirits who had accompanied him throughout his life: Goethe. Although he had published occasional short pieces in which Goethe had played a key role, this is the first and only monograph he devoted to the great German polymath.

The reader quickly notes the extent to which a lifetime of reading Goethe had rendered Hadot intimately familiar with every aspect of his wide-ranging work. For although Hadot's main area of speciality was, of course, the history of Greek and Latin philosophy, he stood out from most of his French contemporaries by his thorough familiarity with German literature: thus, he published articles on Kant and Nietzsche and initially thought of writing a doctoral dissertation on Rilke and Heidegger. Throughout his life, however, Goethe, several editions of whose complete works lined the bookshelves of the home Hadot shared with his German-born wife, Ilsetraut, in Limours, France, held a special place in his heart. This was especially true of the older Goethe, as he appears especially in the *Conversations with Eckermann,* that work, consisting of interviews with Goethe over the last nine years of his life, which Nietzsche famously called "the best German book there is." As he grew older and faced the prospect of death, Hadot increasingly found strength and hope in Goethe's calm acceptance of his own personal mortality and, above all, in his unabated love of life.

To a certain extent, Goethe's intellectual development shows some parallels to Hadot's own. After his youthful Sturm und Drang period, with its glorification of the tempestuous, individualistic, Romantic genius, and trying his hand at almost every literary genre and area of learning, Goethe gradually came to see the value and necessity of dedicating oneself to a life of service to others. In a similar way, Hadot, who had begun by working on the mystical philosophy of Plotinus and the abstruse theology and metaphysics of Marius Victorinus and Porphyry of Tyre, gradually turned toward the study of those Hellenistic philosophers, such as the later Stoics Marcus Aurelius and Epictetus, who focused on more practical questions, such as how we should live our lives. Thanks in part to the influence of his beloved wife, Ilsetraut, Hadot came to see philosophy more and more as a way of life, the purpose and justification of which was to inspire as broad a circle of readers as possible to transform themselves, with a view to leading a flourishing life that was rich, full, and authentic. The means to this goal, Hadot believed, was the practice of what he famously called "spiritual exercises," techniques of self-transformation which, he believed, constituted the essence of philosophy and could still, when suitably modified, do so today. Thus, it seems perfectly appropriate that, near the end of his life, he should return to the study of the practice of spiritual exercises in one of his most beloved authors, Goethe. He no doubt believed that Goethe served as a perfect exemplar of the results to which the lifelong, assiduous practice of such exercises could lead: a rich, full, active, and productive life lived with full appreciation of the infinite value of every moment, combined with an unconditional acceptance of even the seemingly difficult and tragic aspects of human existence.

As compared with my previous translations of Hadot's books, the present work presented new challenges, especially when it came to translating Goethe. Following my previous practice, I first produced literal English translations of Hadot's French versions of Goethe's texts, and then compared them with the original German. The results were often quite different from the French translations used by Hadot, some of which were quite old and sometimes departed considerably from what I take to have been the meaning of Goethe's original texts. In the past, when such divergences occurred, I would get together with Pierre Hadot, and the two of us would reach compromise solutions. Sadly, this was no longer an option, but I have sought a middle ground between faithfulness to the original German and faithfulness to Hadot's interpretation of Goethe's words and thought. The result may not always be aesthetically pleasing—I am no poet and have made no attempt to reproduce the rhymes and rhythms of Goethe's incomparable verse. Yet I hope Pierre Hadot himself would not have considered the result a betrayal.

Michael Chase
Victoria, Canada, January 2022

Preface

Goethe has always been one of my favorite authors. It was time to collect several of the studies I have devoted to him in one publication, while rethinking them.[1] This, then, is the origin of this book, which ultimately refers to the practice in Goethe of what I have called "spiritual exercises," inspired by ancient philosophy, but taken up and developed by a long tradition in Western philosophy.

The expression "spiritual exercise," which has been used by some historians of thought, such as Louis Gernet and Jean-Pierre Vernant, or authors, such as Georges Friedmann, does not have a religious connotation, whatever some critics may believe. They are acts of the intellect, or of the imagination, or of the will, that are characterized by their goal: by means of them, the individual tries to transform her way of seeing the world, in order to transform herself. The point is not to inform, but to form oneself.

To begin, I will study the exercise, dear to Goethe, of concentration on the present instant, which allows us to intensely live each moment of existence without letting ourselves be distracted by the weight of the past or the mirage of the future.

The second chapter refers to another exercise: the view from above, which consists in distancing oneself from things and events and trying to see them from an overall perspective, detaching oneself from one's individual, particular, and partial viewpoint. This exercise can be purely imaginative, but it can also correspond to a physical action, like climbing a mountain.

The third chapter is devoted to the exegesis of the poem *Originary Words* (*Urworte*), which is a description of human destiny. This time, the spiritual exercise is situated at the level of hope, the figure that crowns the poem and, for Goethe, represents a fundamental attitude.

Throughout these three chapters, we can observe one constant attitude in Goethe: amazement at life and existence, despite their painful or terrifying aspects. A fourth chapter is therefore devoted to what I have called the Yes to life and to the world, and to the kinship that exists between Goethe and Nietzsche in this perspective.

Throughout this book, Goethe's deep love for life is expressed, particularly in the poem we shall study later on,[2] in which the *memento mori* (don't forget to die) of the Christians, Platonists, and Romantics is opposed to Goethe's *memento vivere* (don't forget to live), inspired by Spinoza. When Wilhelm Meister, in his *Years of Apprenticeship*,[3] visits the "Room of the past," he reads this motto: "Gedenke zu leben," "Don't forget to live," which is a translation of *memento vivere*.

As I was writing this book, feeling myself growing old, I was haunted by the *memento mori*. Yet under Goethe's influence, I understood the full importance of the *memento vivere*, and then I thought that the Goethean motto "Don't forget to live" could very well epitomize the content of my book and stand as its title.

After having made this choice, I discovered that in 2000, Hans-Jürgen Schings, the great expert on Goethe, had already written an article entitled "Gedenke zu leben. Goethes Lebenskunst" ("Don't forget to live. Goethe's art of living").[4] The author was kind enough to send me his text. This extremely interesting study sets forth Goethe's art of living by means of a psychological and moral analysis of several of Goethe's characters, as well as of the personality of Winckelmann, as it appears in Goethe's praise of the latter.

Faust and Edward, one of the characters of *Elective Affinities*, represent what Goethe's art of living rejects: Faust, because of his inability to concentrate on the present instant, and Edward by his hypochondria and his whims. Opposite them is Winckelmann, a true man of antiquity, who possesses the secret of the art of living, and Wilhelm Meister, who gradually learns to live by devoting himself to action and the service of mankind and to renunciation. The reader will thus discover in Hans-Jürgen Schings's remarkable study many aspects of the art of living according to the author of *Faust* that I have not dealt with in the present work.

I thank first of all Hélène Monsacré, who suggested that I publish this work and obtained precious documents for me. Without the devotion of Concetta Luna, the book could not have been completed; I must express my deepest gratitude to her. Particular thanks also go to Jean-Pierre Fauvet, who collected an abundant documentation for me. I also benefited from the precious assistance and advice of Catherine Balaudé, Novella Bellucci, Herman Bonne, Blanche Buffet, Arnold I. Davidson, Gunter Gebauer, Ilsetraut Hadot, Dieter Harlfinger, Fabienne Jourdan, Birgitta Kessler, Klaus Schöpsdau, and Alain Segonds. My thanks to them all.

Pierre Hadot

1

"The Present Is the Only Goddess I Adore"[1]

Faust and Helen

"Then, the spirit looks neither ahead nor behind. Only the present is our happiness."[2] When Goethe's hero speaks these words in the *Second Faust*, he seems to have reached the culminating point of his "quest for the highest existence."[3] Beside him, on the throne he has had set up for her, is Helen, whose splendid beauty he has glimpsed in the mirror of the sorcerer's kitchen. It was she whom he evoked in the first act, after a frightening journey to the realm of the Mothers, and she with whom he fell madly in love: "Does the source of Beauty, pouring forth so amply, penetrate the depths of my soul? . . . To you I devote all my strength, all my passion, to you, inclination, love, worship, madness."[4] This is the Helen whom he has sought in the second act, throughout all the mythical forms of classical Greece. He has spoken about her with the centaur Chiron and with the sibyl Manto. Finally, in the third act, it is she who has come to take refuge in the medieval fortress, perhaps Mistra in the Peloponnese, of which Faust appears as the lord.

Then the extraordinary encounter takes place between Faust, who, although he appears in the form of a knight of the Middle Ages, is in fact the figure of modern man, and Helen, who, although she is evoked with the features of the heroine of the Trojan War, is in fact the figure of ancient Beauty, and ultimately of the Beauty of Nature. With extraordinary mastery, Goethe has made these figures and symbols come alive, so that the meeting between Faust and Helen is as laden with emotion as the encounter between two lovers, as full of historical meaning as the encounter between two epochs, and as charged with metaphysical meaning as humankind's encounter with its destiny.

The choice of poetic form is used very skillfully to depict both the dialogue of the two lovers and the encounter between two historical epochs. Since the beginning of the third act, Helen had been speaking in the manner of ancient tragedy, and her words were set to the rhythm of the iambic trimeter, while the chorus of captive Trojan women answered her in strophe and antistrophe. Yet as soon as Helen meets Faust and hears the watchman Lynceus express himself in rhymed distichs, she is amazed and charmed by this unknown poetic form: "no sooner has one word struck the ear, than another comes to caress the first."[5] The birth of Helen's love for Faust will be expressed in rhymed distichs, which Faust will begin and Helen will finish, inventing the rhyme each time. By learning this new poetic form, Helen learns, with Faust, to spell out the alphabet of love, as Mephistopheles says.[6] "Then tell me how to express myself so well," Helen begins. "It's very easy," Faust answers, "it must come from the heart. When the breast overflows with longing, one looks around and seeks . . ." "For someone to share our happiness," Helen replies. "Then the spirit looks neither ahead, nor behind—only the present . . ." "Is our happiness," answers Helen. Faust continues: "It is a treasure, highest gain, possession and pledge. But who confirms it?" "My hand," answers Helen.[7] The love duet ends for the time being with the testimony to Helen's abandonment, and the interplay of rhymes thus concludes in a "confirmation" that is not only the echo of the rhyme but also the gift of her hand. Faust and Helen then fall silent and quietly hold one another, while the chorus, adopting the tone of an epithalamium, describes their embrace.

Goethe certainly derived the inspiration for this dialogue of love, which is at the same time a poetic dialogue, from his experience in 1814–15, when he met Marianne von Willemer, an experience that was, moreover, unknown to his contemporaries. When he sent some of his poems from the *West-Eastern Divan* to Marianne, he was surprised to receive from her poems that answered his poems, which he was able to insert into the work. Thus, in the *Book of Suleika*, which is included in this collection, he alludes to the story of the Persian poet who invented rhyme and whose friend answered him by taking up his rhymes. The situation of Faust and Helen is already sketched in the *Divan*: "As gaze responds to gaze, and rhyme to rhyme."[8]

Then the dialogue of love, but also of rhymed verse, begins again between Faust and Helen, letting us experience an instant of such intensity, such resonance, that time seems to stand still, along with the drama. Helen says: "I feel so far away and yet so near, can only happily repeat: I'm here! I'm here!" Faust: "I can scarcely breathe; I tremble, my voice falters. This is a dream: day and place have disappeared." Helen resumes: "I seem to myself worn out, and yet so new; woven together with you, true to the unknown." "Dwell not upon your own fate," Faust replies, "although it be unique among all. Existence is a duty, though it be only for an instant."[9] Here we glimpse the subtle interplay established between magic, dramatic fiction, and reality. The drama seems to stand still. It seems that Helen and Faust have nothing more to desire, so overwhelmed are they by their mutual presence. One thinks of the "Marienbad Elegy": "Nothing was left to you, no wish, no hope, no longing / Here was the goal of your innermost striving."[10]

However, Mephistopheles, who in the second act has donned the monstrous mask of a Phorcyad in order to adapt himself to the Greek world, interrupts this perfect moment by announcing the threatening approach of Menelaus's troops, and Faust upbraids him for his untimely intervention. The wonderful instant has vanished, but the dispositions of Faust and Helen are again reflected in the description of the ideal Arcadia, where Faust and Helen will beget Euphorion, the genius of poetry.

The dialogue we have cited can be understood on several levels. First of all, it is the dialogue between two lovers, who resemble all lovers. Faust and Helen are two lovers absorbed by the living presence of the beloved being, forgetting everything, past and future, outside of that presence. This excess of happiness gives them the impression of something unreal, or of a dream: time and place disappear.

On a second level of interpretation, however, the dialogue takes place between Faust and Helen, who are symbolic figures: of modern humankind in its ceaseless striving, and of ancient beauty in its soothing presence, miraculously united by the magic of poetry, which abolishes the centuries. In this dialogue, a modern man tries to make Helen forget her past, so that she may be entirely in the present instant, which she cannot understand. She feels herself to be so distant and so close, abandoned by life and yet in the process of rebirth, living in Faust, mingled with him, trusting in the unknown. Faust asks her not to reflect on her strange destiny, but to accept the new existence that is offered to her. As Dorothea Lohmeyer has astutely remarked, Helen "modernizes herself," so to speak, by adopting rhyme, the symbol of modern interiority, while doubting and reflecting on her destiny, and Faust "antiquizes," speaking as a man of antiquity, when he urges Helen to focus her attention on the present instant and not to waste this instant in hesitant reflection on the past and the future.[11]

For Goethe, this was precisely the characteristic of ancient life and art: to know how to live in the present, to know what he called, as we shall see, "the health of the moment." In the words of Siegfried Morenz, "No one has characterized that particular nature of Greece better than Goethe . . . on the occasion of the dialogue between Faust and Helen, when the German teaches the art of rhyme to the Greek heroine: Then the spirit looks neither ahead nor behind. Only the present is our happiness."[12]

Indeed, if Faust speaks to Helen as a man of antiquity, it is because Helen's presence—that is, the presence of Beauty—opens up for him the presence of nature: for Goethe, Antiquity and Nature go hand in hand. This is why the dialogue between Faust and Helen can be considered on a third level. The encounter with Helen is a meeting with Beauty, with the presence of Nature, but also with ancient wisdom, with the ancient art of living. To the nihilist Faust, who had bet against Mephistopheles that he would never say to the instant, "Stop, you are so beautiful!," the ancient, noble Helen, after the humble Gretchen, reveals the splendor of being, that is, of the present instant, and invites him to say yes to the instant, the world, and to himself.

The Present, the Trivial, and the Ideal

For Goethe, as we said, the ancients knew how to live in the present, in the "health of the moment," instead of getting lost, like the moderns, in yearning for the past and the future. He develops this idea with all the clarity one could wish in a letter to Zelter,[13] dating from 1829. First of all, he regrets the absence of the letter's addressee, his friend the musician Zelter. On this occasion, he undertakes a meditation on the present and presence, both notions, temporal actuality and spatial proximity, being expressed by the same word *Gegenwart* in German:

> There is really something absurd about Presence. One imagines that's it, now: one sees oneself, one feels oneself. One goes no further. But one has no idea of the benefit one may derive from such moments. We wish to express ourselves on this as follows: The absent person is an ideal person, whereas the people who are present seem completely trivial to one another. It is utterly bizarre that, through the reality of Presence, the ideal is virtually suppressed. This is probably why their ideal appears to the moderns only as longing.

In the following lines, Goethe alludes to the new "way of living" that had become general. In 1829, when he was writing, these

"moderns" he mentions were the Romantics, whose vision of the
world was triumphant in Europe at the time. Longing was fash-
ionable: longing for the absent, distant, inaccessible being; longing
for the past, or the future, or for another world, which would be
elsewhere. This longing for the "ideal" went hand in hand with a
debasement of the real, of everyday reality, of the present, which
the Romantics considered trivial. Goethe rejects this unequivocally.

Not that Goethe was unaware that the present instants of daily life
can become bogged down in what he calls *das Gemeine*,[14] a term that
for him can mean, according to context, what is trivial, common,
ordinary, banal, mechanical, vulgar, mediocre, or platitudinous.
In Goethe's view, the great danger that threatens mankind is to be
unable to rise above triviality and platitude. In a poem in honor of
Schiller, he alludes to the elevation of this poet's soul above this
state of mediocrity:

> Meanwhile, his spirit strode mightily on
> In the eternity of the true, the good, the beautiful,
> And, behind him, in insubstantial appearance,
> lay what dominates us all: the trivial.[15]

Again, in the *Journeyman Years*, he evokes the man who has risen
to his highest summit and can keep himself at that height, "without
being drawn back into platitude by pride or by egoism."[16]

One could perhaps say that, for Goethe, *das Gemeine* is that which
is not illuminated by the Idea, whether it is the Idea immanent in the
laws of nature, or the Idea immanent in the moral laws.[17] A vulgar
and trivial life is a life without ideals, a routine dominated by habit,
worries,[18] egotistic interests, which conceal from us the splendor of
existence. To free oneself from the trivial and from platitude, one
must not, according to Goethe, do as the Romantics did and escape
the present to take refuge in an ideal, whether distant or future.
On the contrary, one must recognize that each present instant is
not trivial, that one must discover its wealth and value, and discern

the presence of the ideal in it, either because it actually is rich and significant in the intensity of the experience it enables one to live, or else because it can be given a moral value by answering the demands of duty, or because poetry or art is able to idealize it. Only by means of this becoming aware of the value of the present can life rediscover its dignity and nobility. It is this vision of the ideal in the real[19] that Goethe found in the paintings of Claude Lorrain, but especially in ancient art: for the ancients, in his view, the real was, as it were, an "idealized reality."[20]

In the letter to Zelter from October 1829 that we have already quoted, Goethe briefly evokes the copies made by the painter F. W. Ternite of the wall paintings of Pompeii and Herculaneum, which brings him back to the theme of presence and the present, simultaneously temporal actuality and coexistence in the universe, two notions that, as we said, are evoked for him by the German word *Gegenwart*:

> This is what is most wondrous in Antiquity for whoever can see with his eyes: that is, the health of the moment and what it is worth. For these paintings, buried in the most horrible catastrophe, are still as fresh, after nearly two thousand years, as robust, as comfortable as in the moment of happiness and contentment that preceded their terrible burial. Asked what they represent, one might be hard pressed to answer. For the moment, I would say the following: these figures give us the feeling that the instant must be pregnant with meaning and self-sufficient, in order to become a worthy incision in time and eternity.[21]

Works of ancient art thus reveal to Goethe two aspects of the attitude of the ancient soul toward the present. First of all, the sense of the "instant pregnant with meaning," or what the Greeks called *kairos*, the moment that one must seize and represent in order to make the past and future visible within it. This was what the sculptor of the "tomb of the dancer" did, of which Goethe speaks in a letter to Sickler:

The beautiful agility with which the dancer moves from one
figure to another, at which we marvel in such artists, is fixed for a
moment, so that we see the past, present, and future at the same
time, and this is enough to transport us to a supraterrestrial state.[22]

With regard to the representation of the moment in the *Laocoon*,
Goethe remarks,

If a work of art is really to move before the eye, a moment of
transition must be chosen: shortly before, no part of the whole
can have been in that position; shortly afterward, each part must
be forced to abandon that position. In this way, the work will be
newly alive, again and again, before millions of spectators.[23]

In general, this choice of the decisive moment in ancient works
of art presupposes intense attention to the present moment and to
its meaning; to the role it plays in the unfolding of events and the
development of processes.[24]

Yet ancient works of art also reveal another aspect of presence
to Goethe. This is no longer merely the perception of the decisive
moment and of the present instant, but also a deep sense of the
value of life, of the living "presence" of beings and things, a poetic
vision that knows how to grasp the ideal within simple reality. This
is what Goethe had felt during his trip to Italy, while looking at
funeral steles at Verona:

The wind that wafts from the tombs of the ancients arrives fra-
grant, as if over a hill of roses. The graves are sincere and touch-
ing, and always produce life. Here is a man who, next to his wife,
looks out of a niche, as if he were at a window. Here are a mother
and father, with their son between them, looking at each other
with ineffable naturalness. Here, a couple stretches out their
hands to each other. Here, a father lying on his couch seems to
be entertained by his family. The immediate "presence" of these

stones was extremely moving to me. They come from later art, but are simple, natural, and generally appealing. No armor-clad man is kneeling here, waiting for a joyful resurrection. More or less skillfully, the artist has portrayed the simple "presence" of human beings, thereby prolonging their existence and making it lasting. They do not join their hands together, do not look toward heaven, but they are, in this world, what they were and what they are. They stand together, take an interest in one another, love one another, and this is expressed in the stones, albeit with a certain lack of manual skill, in a most delightful way.[25]

To express this "health" with which the poets and artists of antiquity described the presence of things, Goethe used a happy formulation: they represented existence, whereas the moderns are interested only in the effect produced by their description:

As far as Homer is concerned, it seems that a veil has fallen from my eyes. The descriptions, similes, and so on seem to us to be poetic, and yet they are ineffably natural, but of course they are sketched with a purity and depth that are frightening. Even the most strangely invented stories have a natural quality that I have never felt in this way, except in the proximity of the objects described. Allow me to briefly express what I mean as follows. They [the ancients] represented existence: we moderns usually represent effects; they described what is terrible, we describe terribly; they described what is pleasant; we describe pleasantly, and so on. This is the origin of all that is exaggerated, all the mannerism, all the false grace, all the bombast. For when one works on effects for the sake of effects, one thinks one cannot make it noticeable enough. Although what I say is not new, I have nevertheless felt it quite intensely on a new occasion. Now that all these coasts and foothills, these gulfs and coves, these islands and capes, cliffs and sandy beaches, bushy hills, gentle meadows, fertile fields, ornamented gardens, well-kept trees, hanging vines, mountains of clouds and ever-bright plains, precipices, sandbanks, and the sea that surrounds everything with so many alternations and diversities are present to my mind, the *Odyssey* is for the first time a living word for me.[26]

Idyllic Arcadia

To the woman he invited to recognize "the only happiness" in the present, Faust proposes to return to her fatherland, the land where she was born:

When, to the murmur of Eurotas' reeds,
She broke forth, radiant, from her shell.[27]

It was by the river Eurotas that Zeus, in the form of a swan, united with Leda, who laid an egg from which Helen emerged. This land is Arcadia, the symbol, for Goethe, of the liberty and joy of primitive nature, the Golden Age,[28] to which Helen naturally belongs by her divine birth. Here, Helen will rediscover at the same time her rootedness within reality and the health of life in the present:

This is what you and I have reached.
Let the past be left behind us!
Oh! Feel that you were sprung from the highest God.
To the first world alone
(that is, to the Golden Age) do you belong.[29]

From its sun-drenched summits to the green fields of its valleys, all of Arcadia, as described by Faust, is filled with a harmonious, pure life. One cannot tell whether its inhabitants are human beings or gods, but one can say of them:

Here, the feeling of well-being is mankind's birthright,
Cheeks are as bright as mouths,

THE PRESENT IS THE ONLY GODDESS I ADORE"

Each is immortal in his place;
All are happy and healthy.[30]

It is in the form of this idyllic Arcadia, this Golden Age, that
Goethe imagines ancient life; and this portrait of the freedom of
Arcadia, which is just as much the description of an inner state,
allows us to glimpse one of the directions in which Goethe's affirmation of the value of the instant in the ancient world is oriented.

In general, this idyllic representation of ancient Greece, tinged
with nostalgia for the divinities of paganism, was in fashion during Goethe's youth. The "Gods of Greece," of whom Schiller sang,
demanded that human beings be joyful:

Gloomy seriousness and sad renunciation
Were banished from your bright worship.
All hearts were to beat in happiness,
For the happy being was akin to you.
Then, nothing was as sacred as the Beautiful.[31]

For Schiller and Hölderlin, the drama of the modern world is that
"the gods have departed, taking with them all that was beautiful, all
that was noble."[32] Yet Hölderlin prophesied:

Until, awakened from the anxious dream, the human soul
will rise, young and joyful, and the blessed breath of love
will once again, as oft before, among the blossoming children of
     Greece,
waft in a new time, upon brows more free,
and the Spirit of Nature, wandering back from afar, will once more
appear to us: the god, lingering quietly in golden clouds.[33]

The work of the great J. Winckelmann made a powerful con-
tribution to this idealization of Greece, which can be observed in
Goethe, Schiller, and Hölderlin. The essay that Goethe devoted

to Winckelmann is highly revealing in this regard. In his view, Winckelmann himself becomes a man of antiquity and a pagan, that is, a happy, healthy man, living in the present, whose serene figure he opposes to the sickly, Christian worry of the Romantics. Whereas modern man hurls himself almost constantly into the infinite,

> the Ancients felt directly and immediately that their only well-being lay within the lovely limits of such a beautiful world. Here they had been placed, here they were called, here they found room for their activity, here their passion found its objects and its nourishment.[34]

What makes the grandeur of the poetry and history of antiquity is that they placed onstage characters who had an intense interest in the realities that were closest to them: themselves, their country, the life of their fellow citizens; that is, "they acted on the present." This is why it could not be difficult for the author, who was similarly disposed, to make such a present eternal:

> The only thing that had value for them was what actually happened, in the same way as for us, only what is thought or felt seems to have value . . . they kept to what is nearby, true, and real. Even the images of their imaginations had bones and marrow![35]

For Goethe, as he continues to sketch the portrait of Winckelmann, the ancient spirit and the pagan spirit were closely linked. Their common features were self-confidence, action in the present, admiration of the gods as works of art, and submission to higher destiny.

It was characteristic of ancient humankind to rejoice spontaneously and unconsciously at their own existence, without, as the moderns do, making a detour through reflection and language. Such, in Goethe's view, is precisely what ancient health is. He would certainly have been willing to consider, like Plotinus,[36] that this health is unconscious, because it is in conformity with nature, while consciousness corresponds to a state of disturbance of illness. The more an activity is pure and intense, the less it is conscious.

Unconscious Health or Conquered Serenity?

As Klaus Schneider rightly emphasized, "The definition of the essence of Hellenism, that is, for Winckelmann, of the ideal human being or of divine perfection, as 'noble simplicity and calm majesty,' is taken from the interpretation of works of fine art,"[37] particularly those of the fourth century BCE, which the famous archaeologist had proposed.[38] Yet this interpretation does not take the literary works of antiquity into account. This idyllic representation of Greek life as imagined by Winckelmann and Goethe was, moreover, criticized from quite an early date. As early as 1817, the great philologist August Boeckh wrote: "The Greeks were more unhappy than many believe."[39] In *The World as Will and Representation*, Schopenhauer cites texts from lyric and tragic poets that reveal the profound pessimism of the Greeks:

> The most enviable of all good things on earth is not to have been born at all, and never to have seen the burning rays of the sun; if one is born, to pass as early as possible through the gates of Hades, and to rest under a thick mantle of earth.[40]

Yet it was above all Jacob Burckhardt, and following him, Nietzsche, who vigorously criticized the ideas of Winckelmann and Goethe in the course of the nineteenth century.[41]

It is true that this idyllic representation of Greek spontaneous joy and health hardly corresponded, in fact, to historical reality. Ancient humans were just as worried and just as anguished as modern ones. Like us, they bore the burden of the past, the worries and hopes of the future, and the fear of death. Hesiod speaks of the "sad cares"[42] that torture human beings since Pandora opened the jar of evils, closing its cover upon hope. The lot of the human race in its current state, the race of iron, is "during the day, fatigue and misery; and at night, the harsh anguish [*merimnai*] sent by the gods."[43] The lyric and tragic poets echo him: "Nor is any human blessed, but all mortals whom the sun looks down upon are in a sorry state."[44] "Ah, generations of men, how close to nothingness I esteem your life to be!"[45]

Goethe admired the "health of the moment" in the paintings of Pompeii and Herculaneum. However, at about the same time, Horace spoke of "black Anxiety" who rides inexorably behind a horseman,[46] and Lucretius denounced mankind's inner worry:

> Just as men seem to feel that there is a weight on their minds which tries them with its heaviness, if so they could also recognize from what causes it comes, and what makes so great a mountain of misery lie upon their chest, they would not lead their lives as now we generally see them do, each not knowing what he wants, each seeking always to change his place as if he could drop his burden . . . Thus each person flees from himself, but to that self, from which of course he can never escape, he clings against his will, and hates it.[47]

Long before Pascal's analysis of boredom, the ancients had felt this inner void, this self-hatred, this anguish at being alone with oneself that characterize human beings. Seneca wrote an extraordinary page in which he analyzes such illnesses of the soul[48] as "self-hatred," "the pleasure one feels at tormenting oneself and making oneself suffer," "the boiling of the soul that cannot settle on anything," "the disgust at life and the universe."[49]

One can assume, moreover, that Goethe was too familiar with ancient literature to be unaware that care and anguish, which are, as it were, the stuff of human life, were already the lot of human beings at that time. Yet he considered that ancient serenity was so strong that "in the highest instants of pleasure, as well as in the deepest moments of sacrifice, or even of destruction, the ancients maintained an indestructible health."[50] One might think that this serenity was self-evident, that it was inherent in the Greek temperament. Yet as Nietzsche saw, this serenity was acquired, not primitive, and was the result of an immense effort of will. For him, this was an aesthetic will to throw the dazzling veil of artistic creation over the horrors of existence.[51] Above all, however, there existed in antiquity a philosophical will to find peace of mind by the transformation of oneself and of one's gaze at the world.

The Philosophical Experience of the Present

This philosophical will was already sketched in the archaic period. When Pittakos, one of the Seven Sages, declares that the best thing is to "do the present well,"[52] that is, to concentrate on the present—which implies that one should not let oneself be distracted by the past and the future—it is indeed a piece of advice and a rule of behavior that is being proposed.

In the Sophistic movement of the fifth century BCE, which offered young Athenians training for political life, we can see that Antiphon the Sophist, for example, criticized his contemporaries for, so to speak, giving up what they have for something far less certain, by failing to live in the present, which is the only reality:

> There are some people who do not live the present life but make preparations with great effort, as though they were going to live some different life, and not the present one. And while they are doing this, the time that they are neglecting is gone . . . it is not possible to retract one's life like a move in checkers.[53]

It was said that Aristippus, one of Socrates's followers, "knew how best to manage the present situation,"[54] that is, to enjoy present good things without trying to attain absent or inaccessible things, and that he considered that there was happiness only in the present instant.[55]

This attitude inspired admiration, which shows that it did not correspond to a generalized, spontaneous behavior but on the contrary was the result of a conscious, deliberate philosophical will to adapt oneself to reality as it presents itself.

Despite the profound difference between Stoic and Epicurean doctrines, one can discern, underlying the two doctrines, an important analogy in the experience of the present. It can be defined as follows: Epicureanism and Stoicism privilege the present over the past, and especially over the future. They made it a principle that happiness must be found in the present alone, that an instant of happiness is equivalent to an eternity of happiness, and that happiness can and must be found immediately, right now, at once. Epicureanism and Stoicism invite us to resituate the present moment within the perspective of the cosmos and to attribute an infinite value to the slightest moment of existence.

Epicureanism was above all a therapeutics of anxiety. People are terrified because they believe that the gods concern themselves with human beings and hold punishments in store for them after death. They are troubled by the fear of death, devoured by the cares and sufferings engendered by unsatisfied desires. For some, there is the moral worry brought about by the concern to act with perfect purity of intention. The practice of Epicureanism was intended to deliver humankind from these multiple torments. The gods themselves live in perfect tranquility, without being troubled by the care of producing the universe or governing it, for this universe is the mechanical result of an encounter between atoms that exist eternally; the gods therefore pose no threat to human beings. The soul does not survive the body, and death is not an event of life; it therefore means nothing to humankind. Desires trouble us only if they are artificial and useless: one must reject those that are neither natural nor necessary, prudently satisfy those that are natural but not necessary, and satisfy, above all, the desires that are indispensable for the survival of existence. As far as moral worries are concerned, they will be completely appeased if one does not hesitate to acknowledge that humans, like all living beings, are always guided by pleasure. If one seeks wisdom, it is simply because it brings peace of mind, that is, ultimately, a state of pleasure. Epicureanism proposes a wisdom that teaches one to relax, to suppress worry, a wisdom that, moreover, is only apparently easy, for one must renounce many things in order to desire only what one is certain to obtain and to submit one's desires to the judgment of reason. The goal, in fact, is a complete transformation of life, and one of the main aspects of this transformation is a change in attitude with regard to time.

For the Epicureans, senseless people—that is, most of the human race—are devoured by insatiable desires aimed at wealth, glory, power, and the disorderly pleasures of the flesh.[56] What characterizes all these desires is that they cannot be satisfied in the present. This is why, as the Epicureans said, senseless people "do not recollect their past nor enjoy their present blessings; they merely look forward to those of the future, and since these are necessarily uncertain, they are consumed with anxiety and terror. The worst of their torment is when they perceive too late that they have devoted their zeal in vain to money, power, wealth, or glory. For they never attain any of the pleasures for which they had been inflamed by hope, and for the conquest of which they had worked so hard."[57] "The fool's life is unpleasant and anxious," according to an Epicurean saying; "it rushes entirely toward the future."[58]

Thus, Epicurean wisdom did indeed propose a radical transformation of the human attitude to time, a transformation that had to be effective at each of life's instants. One must know how to enjoy present pleasures without letting oneself be distracted from them, avoiding thinking about the past, if it is unpleasant, or about the future, insofar as it provokes disorderly fears or hopes in us. Only the thought of what is pleasant, of pleasure, whether past or future, is allowed into the present moment, especially when the goal is to compensate for present pain. This transformation presupposes a specific conception of pleasure, according to which the quality of pleasure depends neither on the quantity of desires it satisfies, nor on the duration in which it is realized.

The quality of pleasure does not depend on the quantity of desires it satisfies. The best and the most intense pleasure is that which is the least mixed with worry, and which most certainly ensures peace of mind. It will therefore be obtained by the satisfaction of natural and necessary desires, the essential desires necessary for the preservation of existence. But these desires can be easily satisfied without any need to expect them from the future, with no need to yield to the uncertainty and worry of a long pursuit. "Thanks be to blessed Nature," says an Epicurean sentence, "that she made necessary things easy to obtain, and things hard to obtain not necessary."[59] All kinds of illness of the soul—human passion, desires for wealth, power, or depravity–force us to think of the past or the future. Yet the purest and most intense pleasure can be easily obtained in the present.

Not only does pleasure not depend on the quantity of satisfied desires, but above all, it does not depend on duration. It does not need to be long in order to be absolutely perfect. "An infinite time cannot provide us with a pleasure greater than that with which the time which we know is finite provides us."[60]

This may seem to be a paradox, which is based first of all on a theoretical idea. The Epicureans thought of pleasure as a reality in itself that is not situated in the category of time. Aristotle had already said that pleasure is complete and total at each moment of its duration, and that its prolongation does not change its essence.[61] For the Epicureans, a practical attitude is added to this theoretical representation. By limiting itself to what ensures complete peace of mind, pleasure reaches a summit that cannot be transcended, and it is impossible to increase this pleasure by duration. Pleasure is entirely within the present instant, and one does not have to wait for anything at all from the future in order to increase it.

One could summarize everything we have just said by these verses from Horace: "Let the soul find its pleasure in the present and come to hate worries about what is beyond."[62] A happy mind does not look toward the future. We can be happy right now, if we limit our desires reasonably.

Not only can we do this, but we must. Yes, happiness can be found immediately, right now, in the present. Instead of reflecting on the whole of one's life, calculating hopes and uncertainties, one must seize happiness in the present instant. The matter is urgent: "We were born only once," says an Epicurean sentence, "twice is not allowed. We must therefore be no more for eternity. But you, who are not the master of tomorrow, you put off joy until tomorrow. And yet, life is consumed in vain in procrastination, and each one of us dies without having known peace."[63] "While we are speaking," says Horace, "jealous time has fled. Seize the day [*carpe diem*], then, and trust tomorrow as little as possible."[64]

Horace's *carpe diem* is by no means, as is often imagined, the advice of a sensualist. On the contrary, it is an invitation to conversion, that is, to becoming aware of the vanity of superfluous, limitless desires. It also means becoming aware of the imminence of death, of the uniqueness of life and of the instant. In this perspective, each instant appears as a wonderful gift that fills whoever receives it with gratitude: "Believe," says Horace once again, "that each new day that dawns will be the last for you. Then you will receive each unexpected hour with gratitude."[65]

Gratitude, amazement: we have already encountered these feelings among the Epicureans, in the context of the miraculous coincidence between the needs of a living being and the facilities Nature provides for it. The secret of Epicurean joy and serenity is to live each day as if it were the last, but also as if it were the first. One feels the same grateful amazement by greeting the instant as if it were unexpected as by greeting it as completely new. In the words of Lucretius:

If all things were now revealed for the first time to mortals, if they were thrown before them suddenly and unexpectedly, what more wonderful than these things could be said, or which people would have less dared to believe beforehand?[66]

Ultimately, the secret of Epicurean joy and serenity is the experience of infinite pleasure provided by the awareness of existing, even if only for an instant. To show that a single instant of existence is enough to provide this infinite pleasure, the Epicureans practiced saying every day: "I have had all the pleasure I could have expected." As Horace says: "That man will be master of himself and live a happy life who as each day ends can say 'I have lived.' "[67] Here again, we see the role of the thought of death in Epicureanism. To say, every evening, "I have lived"—that is, "my life is over"—is to practice the same exercise that consisted in saying: "today will be the last day of my life." Yet it is precisely this exercise of becoming aware of life's finitude that reveals the infinite value of the pleasure of existing in the instant. In the perspective of death, the fact of existing, even if only for a moment, suddenly assumes an infinite value and provides a pleasure of infinite intensity. One can say "my life is over" and remain unperturbed only if one has become aware of the fact that one has already had everything in that moment of existence.

All this must, moreover, be resituated within the context of a general vision of the universe. Thanks to the doctrine of Epicurus, which explains the origin of the universe by the fall of atoms in the void, in the eyes of a philosopher, as Lucretius says, the walls of the world open up, and all things appear in the immense void, in the immensity of the All.[68] Like Metrodorus, the Epicurean can exclaim: "Remember that, being mortal by nature, with a limited life, you have risen by the reasonings about nature to the infinity and eternity of things, and you have seen all that has been and all that will be."[69]

Here we find the contrast between finite time and infinite time. In finite time, the sage grasps all that occurs in infinite time. More precisely, as Léon Robin said, commenting on Lucretius: "The sage places himself in the immutability, independent of time, of eternal Nature."[70] Thus, the Epicurean sage perceives, in this awareness of existence, the totality of the cosmos. Nature, as it were, gives him everything in the instant.

In Stoicism, the moment of concentration on the present is even more accentuated, as is clearly apparent in this meditation of Marcus Aurelius:

The following are enough for you:

The judgment you are emitting in this moment on reality, as long as it is objective,

The action you are carrying out at this moment, as long as it is accomplished for the service of the human community,

The inner disposition in which you are in this very moment, as long as it is a disposition of joy in the face of every conjuncture of events brought about by external causality.[71]

Marcus Aurelius thus practices concentrating his attention on the present moment, that is, on what he is thinking, doing, and feeling in this very moment. "This is enough for you," he says to himself, and the expression has a double meaning: this is enough to keep you busy, you don't need to think about anything else; and this is enough to make you happy, there's no need to seek anything else. This is the exercise he himself calls "delimiting the present."[72] To delimit the present is to divert one's attention from the past and the future, in order to concentrate it on what one is in the process of doing.

The present Marcus Aurelius is talking about is a present defined by the lived contents of human consciousness: it thus represents a certain thickness of time, a thickness that corresponds to the attention of lived consciousness.[73] It is this lived present, relative to consciousness, that is in play when Marcus Aurelius advises us to "delimit the present." This is an important point: the present is defined with regard to the thought and action of the person who commits her entire personality to it.

The present suffices for our happiness because it is the only thing that belongs to us and depends on us. In the view of the Stoics, it is essential to know how to distinguish between what depends on us and what does not depend on us. The past no longer depends on us, because it is fixed definitively, while the future does not depend on us because it does not yet exist. Only the present depends on us. It is therefore the only thing that can be good or bad, because it is the only thing that depends on our will. Because they do not depend on us, and do not pertain to the order of moral good or evil, the past and the future must be indifferent to us. There is no use worrying about what no longer exists or what may never be.

Marcus Aurelius also describes this exercise of delimiting the present as follows:

> If you separate from yourself, that is, from your thought . . . all that you have done or said in the past, and all the things that worry you because they have yet to occur . . . ; if you separate from time what is beyond the present and what is past . . . and if you practice living only the life that you live—that is, the present—you will be able to spend all the time left to you until your death, with calm, benevolence, and serenity.[74]

Similarly, Seneca describes this exercise as follows:

> One must circumscribe two things: the fear of the future and the memory of past difficulties: the latter no longer concerns me, while the former does not concern me yet . . . The sage enjoys the present without depending on the future. Freed from the heavy cares that torture the soul, he hopes for nothing, desires nothing, and does not launch himself into what is doubtful, for he is content with what he has [that is, with the present, the only thing that belongs to us]. Do not believe that he is content with little, for what he has [the present] is everything.[75]

Here, we witness the same transfiguration of the present that we encountered in Epicureanism. For the Stoics, we have everything in the present. The present alone is our happiness, for two reasons: First, because, like Epicurean pleasure, Stoic happiness is complete at each instant and does not increase with duration. Next, because in the present instant we possess the whole of reality, and an infinite duration could not give us more than what we possess in the present moment.

In the first place, then, happiness—that is, for the Stoics, moral action or virtue—is always finished, total and complete, at each moment of its duration. Like the Epicurean sage's pleasure, the happiness of the Stoic sage is complete, lacking nothing, as a circle is still a circle, whether it is large or small.[76] Like a propitious or opportune moment, a favorable occasion is an instant whose perfection depends not on duration but precisely on quality, on the harmony that exists between the external situation and the possibilities one has: happiness just is the instant in which a human being is completely in accord with nature.

As for the Epicureans, so for the Stoics, an instant of pleasure is thus equivalent to an eternity. In the words of Chrysippus: "if one is wise even for a moment, one will not be at all inferior in happiness to him who exercises virtue forever."[77]

As for the Epicureans, for the Stoics as well, one will never be happy if one is not happy immediately. It is now or never. The matter is urgent: death is imminent, one must hurry, and one needs nothing in order to be happy other than to want to be so. The past and the future are of no use. What is needed is to immediately transform our way of thinking, acting, and greeting events, in order to think according to the truth, act according to justice, and greet events with love. As for the Epicurean, so for the Stoic, it is the imminence of death that gives the present instant its value. As Marcus Aurelius says, "One must accomplish every act of life as if it were the last."[78] Then each instant takes on all its seriousness, all its value, all its splendor, and we clearly see the vanity of that which we were pursuing with so much worry and which death will snatch away from us. We must live each day with an attention so intense that we can say to oneself every evening, "I have lived," that is, "I have realized my life, I have had all that I could expect from life." In the words of Seneca: "He who has lived his entire life every day possesses peace of mind."[79]

We have just seen the first reason why the present alone suffices for our happiness: it is because one instant of happiness is equivalent to an entire eternity of happiness. The second reason is that in one instant, we possess the totality of the universe. The present instant is fleeting and minuscule—Marcus Aurelius insists strongly on this point[80]—but in this flash, as Seneca says, we can proclaim, along with God: "Everything belongs to me."[81] The instant is our sole point of contact with reality, but it offers us all of reality. Precisely because it consists in passage and metamorphosis, it lets us participate in the general movement of the event of the world and the reality of the world's becoming.

To understand this, one must recall what moral action, virtue, or wisdom represents for the Stoic. Moral good, which is the only good for the Stoic, has a cosmic dimension: it means harmonizing the reason within us with the Reason that governs the cosmos, and produces the concatenation of fate. At each moment, it is our judgment, our action, our desires that must be harmonized with universal Reason. In particular, we must joyfully greet the conjuncture of events that results from the course of Nature. At every instant, therefore, we must resituate ourselves within the perspective of universal Reason, so that at each instant, our consciousness can become a cosmic consciousness. Thus, at every instant, if human beings live in harmony with universal Reason, their consciousness is dilated into the infinity of the cosmos, and the entire cosmos is present to them. This is possible because, for the Stoics, there is a total mixture, or a reciprocal implication of all things within all things. Chrysippus spoke of a drop of wine that becomes mixed with the entire ocean and extends to the whole world.[82]

"He who sees the present moment," says Marcus Aurelius, "has seen all that has occurred from all eternity, and all that will happen in the infinity of time."[83] This is what explains the attention given to each present event, to what happens to us at every instant. The entire world is implied in every event:

> What happens to you has been prepared in advance for you from eternity, and the interweaving of causes has, since forever, woven together your substance and the encounter with that event.[84]

THE PRESENT IS THE ONLY GODDESS I ADORE"   25

Here we could speak of a mystical dimension of Stoicism. At each moment, at each instant, one must say yes to the universe, that is, to the will of universal Reason. One must want what universal Reason wants, that is, the present instant such as it is. Some Christian mystics have also described their state as that of a continuous consent to God's will. Marcus Aurelius exclaims: "I say to the universe: I love along with you."[85] This is a deep feeling of participation, identification, and belonging to an All that transcends the individual's limits, a feeling of intimacy with the universe. For Seneca, the sage plunges into the cosmos (*toti se inserens mundo*).[86] The sage lives in the consciousness of the world, and the world is always present to him. Even more than in Epicureanism, the present moment thus takes on an infinite value: it contains within itself the entire cosmos, all the value and richness of being.

It is therefore quite remarkable that these two schools, Stoic and Epicurean, which were so opposed to one another, both place the concentration of consciousness on the present moment at the center of their way of life. The difference between the two schools resides only in the fact that the Epicurean enjoys the present moment, whereas the Stoic wills it intensely. For one it is a pleasure; for the other, a duty.

The Tradition of Ancient Philosophy in Goethe

One may wonder whether Goethe knew these traditions of ancient philosophy. Although he had read Seneca, Epictetus, and Marcus Aurelius, he does not cite them with regard to attention to the present. Nevertheless, in a conversation with Falk,[87] he speaks of certain beings who, by their innate tendencies, are half Stoic, half Epicurean. He was not surprised, he said, at the fact that they accept the basic principles of the two systems at the same time, or even that they strive to combine them as much as possible. One could say that as far as the present is concerned, Goethe himself was half Stoic, half Epicurean. He knew how to enjoy the present like an Epicurean, and he willed it intensely like a Stoic. The entire literary tradition, moreover, from Montaigne down to the "popular" philosophy of the eighteenth century,[88] had kept the lessons of ancient wisdom more or less alive. In the seventeenth century, for instance, they are expressed in the poem by Andreas Gryphius (1616–64), often cited when one wished to recommend concentration on the present:

> The years that time has taken from me are not mine
> The years that might perhaps come are not mine,
> The [present] moment is mine, and I give it my attention
> So is that moment mine, which has made the year, and eternity.[89]

In the Fifth Promenade of *The Reveries of a Solitary Walker*, written in 1777, Rousseau echoes the Epicureans and the Stoics by opposing people's habitual attitude to time to his own experience of the present. They seek the pleasure of the moment but are torn by the weight of the past and the fear or hope of the future:

> Our affections that attach to external things necessarily pass and change like them. Always ahead of or behind us, they recall the past that no longer exists, or foresee the future, which often is not to be . . . Thus, in this world, we scarcely have anything but passing pleasures; as for lasting happiness, I doubt that it is known. There is hardly an instant, in our most intense enjoyments, when our heart can truly say to us: I would like this instant to last forever.[90]

Let us note in passing that one might wonder whether we do not find an echo of this formulation in Faust's pact with the devil, where Faust swears never to say: "Remain, instant, you are so fair!" It does seem, however, that Faust, when he speaks of the instant, is thinking about an instant of exceptional quality, not of a simple pleasure.

In opposition to the habitual attitude of human beings, Rousseau describes the experience he had on the Île Saint-Pierre, of a "feeling of existence," of a "happiness that was sufficient, perfect, and full,

that does not leave in the soul any void that it feels the need to fill."
This feeling is not available to everyone, at any time: "The heart must
be at peace, and no passion must come to disturb its calm." It is a
state in which the soul does not "need to recall the past or prolong
itself into the future . . . , in which the present continues to endure,
yet without marking its duration, and without any trace of succession." "What does one enjoy in such a situation? Nothing that is
external to oneself, nothing except oneself and one's own existence,
as long as this state lasts, one is self-sufficient like God."[91] Goethe
may have retained from this text the idea of a feeling so intense that
it frees us from the thought of the past and the future and provides
us with unexpected pleasure. He too speaks of the joy one derives
from being there, or from existing.[92]

The Present, the Instant, and Being-There in Goethe

Let us now return to the meeting between Faust and Helen. Before
we go further, however, we must pause briefly to discuss the different expressions Goethe uses to speak of the present moment,
in order to be able to grasp some nuances of his thought. In the
dialogue between Faust and Helen that we have cited, the only
term mentioned was the present, *Gegenwart*. As W. Schadewaldt
remarks, in Goethe the word *Gegenwart* still retains its original
meaning of "presence," in the sense of appearance, manifestation,
or "being-there" in front of us.[93] It is therefore synonymous with
Dasein, "being-there." One rejoices in presence (*Gegenwart*) or in
being-there (*Dasein*). Yet there is presence, reality, and being-there
only in the "present moment" (*Augenblick*), which is fleeting, but
can, as we shall see, imply the past and the future, insofar as in it we
encounter duration or the becoming of the world. Conversely, there
is an instant only in the living and lived perception of presence: "The
immediate presence of these [grave]stones moved me deeply."[94]
Augen-blick evokes a "blink," the instant of a glance. Goethe was no
doubt thinking of this etymology when he wrote in the "Marienbad

Elegy": "Look the instant [*Augenblick*] in the eye [*Augen*]."[95] This present instant is obviously no infinitesimal division. It is, in fact, a certain thickness of time, which, as we have said,[96] corresponds to the attention of lived consciousness. The present instant has the duration of the event or the action lived by a person in the "present" moment, which provoke in her an emotion or an act of will that involves her as a whole. Goethe, moreover, also uses the word *Moment*, the "moment," to designate the instant.[97]

In addition, two quite different aspects of the instant in Goethe must be distinguished: the exceptional instant of happiness offered by fate, in a sense the "blink" (*Augen-blick*) of fate, and the instant that we might call everyday, to which human beings can and must give meaning. The exceptional instant is an intoxicating moment in which existence is intensified, and in which one reaches a culmination, as in the amorous encounter experienced by Faust and Helen. This instant of ineffable ecstasy[98] gives the impression that time has stood still and that one has achieved eternity. In this exceptional instant of happiness, a person may abandon herself naively, but she may also become aware of all its wealth and its meaning, experience it intensely, interiorize it, and commit herself entirely to it, assuming it by a voluntary gift of herself. When one is invaded by happiness, particularly by the feeling of love, one lets oneself be absorbed by the present unreflectingly and involuntarily. As Goethe writes in a poem addressed to Count Paar: "Happiness looks neither forward nor backward, and thus the instant is eternalized."[99] This is what happens to Faust and Helen, in their mutual bedazzlement: "When the breast overflows with longing, one looks around and searches for someone to share our happiness. Then the spirit looks neither ahead, nor behind—only the present is our happiness." Yet this spontaneous absorption in the present instant can be "confirmed," or interiorized, becoming an act of will and a gift of oneself. This also happens to Faust and Helen, when their rhyming dialogue continues: "It is a treasure, highest gain, possession and pledge. But who confirms it?—My hand." Shortly afterward, when Faust feels that Helen is

THE PRESENT IS THE ONLY GODDESS I ADORE

doubting her own identity in the new existence that is granted to
her, he asks her not to let herself be carried away by vain reflections
on the past: "Dwell not upon your own fate, although it be unique
among all. Existence is a duty, though it be unique among all."[100]
Here, love opens up access to the awareness of existence and to consent to being-in-the-world.[101] This twofold aspect is also expressed
in the *West-Eastern Divan*:

> Great is the joy of being-there [*Freude des Daseins*]
> Greater still is the joy one feels in existence itself [*Freude am
> Dasein*].[102]

In his commentary on these two verses, Erich Trunz explains that
the first verse corresponds to the joy of being-there, that is, to the
naive enjoyment of the instant of happiness given by fate, while the
second one corresponds to the joy one feels in the consciousness
of existence, in the presence of what is.[103] In other words, we might
add, of being-there in the world which, thanks to love, opens up to
human beings and is perceived by them in a new way. To understand
this twofold aspect of the intoxicating instant, one may cite this text
by Boris Pasternak, in which the two moments of the experience
are clearly distinguished:

> Never, never, even in their moments of richest and wildest happi-
> ness, were they unaware of a sublime joy in the total design of the
> universe, a feeling that they themselves were a part of that whole,
> an element in the beauty of the cosmos.[104]

Thus, there would be two possible phases in the experience of a
blessed and exceptional instant: spontaneous and thoughtless joy,
then becoming aware, and the act of will that transforms amorous
ecstasy into consent to being-in-the world. This cosmic nature of
the exceptional instant seems to be well expressed in the beautiful
poem from the *Divan*, *Wiederfinden* (Reunion).[105] The first stanza

seems to express only the joy of a reunion between two lovers, and
it ends with these verses: "At the memory of past pains, I shudder
before the present," which seem to express only the intensity of the
emotion of the reunion. Yet the following stanzas open up a whole
new perspective. They transport us to the origin of the world and
the moment of creation: "A painful 'Alas!' resounded, / When the
universe, with a mighty gesture, / Erupted into realities." Light and
darkness were separated, but thanks to the creation of the dawn and
of colors, they reunite and love one another. The universe is thus
the product of an immense systole and diastole. Now those who are
made for one another seek each other out: "Allah has no more need
to create. It is we who create His universe." The ecstasy of love thus
appears as a cosmic ecstasy.

One might now wonder why Mephistopheles, who has an agreement signed in Faust's blood, stipulating that Faust will belong to him
if he says to the instant: "Stay, you are so fair!," does not declare that he
has won the bet and seize Faust's soul when the latter says: "Only the
present is our happiness." Obviously, the commentators have asked
themselves this question. Some have thought that the instant Faust is
talking about here has nothing in common with the instant that is the
subject of the pact with Mephistopheles.[106] The instant lived by Faust
and Helen is not the pleasure of a moment, but an ineffable experience
of absolute being, transcending duration. Other interpreters consider
that the reason why Mephistopheles does not take advantage of the
opportunity is that in his view, the reunion between Faust and Helen
is purely phantasmagorical and completely foreign to reality. In a pre-
publication, Goethe himself had given this third act of the tragedy
the subtitle "classical-romantic phantasmagoria."[107] Yet one can also
specify this interpretation by saying that if Mephistopheles does not
take advantage of the opportunity, it is because he sees only what is
external here, the effect of his magic powers, without understanding
what is going on inside Faust's soul.[108] Or else, one might wonder, is it
perhaps because Faust does not take up the exact terms he used when
he spoke? Alternatively, because he does not command the instant to

stand still but wants to live with Helen in the future? Or is it because Mephistopheles, who in this third act has been transformed into a Phorcyad, has lost his infernal character?[109]

According to Chancellor von Müller, Goethe often said: "A work of art, and especially a poem, that leaves nothing to be guessed at, is not a true work of art, a work of real value; its highest goal is always to incite the audience to reflect, and the work can only really please the reader or the spectator if it forces him to interpret it according to his own feelings, to continue and complete its creation, as it were."[110] From this viewpoint, it cannot be doubted that the drama of *Faust* is a genuine work of art. To understand this, it suffices to glimpse all the literature that has been devoted to the question of whether, at the end of the play, Mephistopheles has won the bet he made with Faust. Alongside all these uncertainties, however, one thing seems certain to me. When he declares that he will never say to the instant "Stay, you are so fair!" Faust is thinking of an exceptional, intensely lived moment that is a summit of existence. Throughout his adventure, there are only three occasions when he experiences such moments without literally pronouncing the formula.[111] The first is his encounter with Marguerite, when Faust declares: "Let this gaze, this clasped hand tell you what cannot be expressed: to devote oneself entirely, to feel a bliss that must be eternal."[112] The second is the meeting with Helen, and the third takes place at the moment of Faust's death: the hope of causing the emergence of a free people, in a paradisiac land, which makes him say, in the conditional and not in the indicative as was the case in the original wager: if this project were realized, "I could then say to the moment: 'Remain, you are so fair!' . . . in anticipation of such great happiness, I now enjoy the highest moment."[113] These exceptional instants can thus be experienced in love, in the joy of the contemplation of beauty or of nature, or in creative activity.[114] The paradox of these privileged instants offered by fate is that they seem to come to us from outside, and yet they correspond to what is most intimate about us, to what is most properly ours. Marcus Aurelius had said: "Whatever happens to you has been prepared in advance for you from eternity, and the interweaving of causes has, from perpetuity, woven together your substance and the encounter with that event."[115] Goethe seems to echo him in the poem entitled "Property":

I know that nothing belongs to me
But the thought that, unimpeded,
Wants to flow from my soul,
And every favorable moment
Which a loving fate
Lets me enjoy so deeply.[116]

Above all, we have these words reported by Chancellor von Müller, with regard to what had been a great moment, a great event in Goethe's life: his meeting with the pianist Szymanowska. As the time to separate approaches, he criticizes the idea of remembrance (*Er-innerung*):

When something great, beautiful, and significant happens to us, it must not be first recalled from outside [*er-innert*], as if it were being hunted; it must rather be interwoven from the outset into our inner being, become one with it, generate within us a new, better self, and thus live on in and create in us, eternally forming us. There is no past toward which one could look back, only something eternally new that takes shape out of the expanded elements of the past; and true *Sehnsucht* [nostalgia] must be always productive, creating something new and better. And . . . have we not all had this experience in these days? Do we not all feel, all of us, in our innermost being, refreshed, improved, expanded by this charming, noble apparition, which now wishes to leave us? No, it cannot escape us, it has transformed into our most intimate self, it continues to live with us, in us; let it try to escape me as it will, I always hold it within me.[117]

From this fine text, we should note not only that the exceptional instant corresponds, in a way, to our inner becoming, but above all, that it is creative. This, moreover, is, I believe, why in Goethe's view the pact between Faust and Mephistopheles ultimately has no meaning, for any beautiful instant we encounter does not invite us to rest in it, but represents for us a formative novelty that cannot help but incite the self to rise toward higher levels.

In life, however, there are not only these exceptional instants offered to us by fate. There are also all the "everyday" instants. Goethe thought that the ancients lived, naturally as it were, in the present, or the "health of the moment." We have seen that this was a rather utopian viewpoint. Yet one thing was certain for him: that is, that the moderns have lost that precious health. However, certain natures discover it spontaneously, like Egmont, who, in conformity with the joie de vivre that is typical of him, declares: "Should I not enjoy the present instant, in order to be sure of the moment that will follow? And consume that one, too, in cares and moodiness?"[118]

Usually, however, people do not pay attention to the present. As Goethe says in a conversation with Chancellor von Müller: "it is because people do not know how to appreciate and animate the value of the present, that they have yearned so deeply for a better future, and flirted so much with the past."[119]

Like the ancient philosophers, Goethe thus tries to react against this attitude, which, for him as for them, constitutes mankind's unhappiness. For him, concentrating on the present moment is a "rule of life," as he says in the poem that bears this very title:

Would you build yourself a lovely life?
You must not fret about the past
Be disgruntled as little as possible
You must always enjoy the present
Above all, hate no man,
and leave the future to God.[120]

Here we find once again the attitude we have described: not to care about the past, not to fret about the future. It has a certain

Epicurean tone—to enjoy the present—but also Stoic, not to say Christian: to accept the will of providence. We find the same connection between happiness, forgetting the past, and entrusting the future to the care of providence in this meditation by Marcus Aurelius: "All this happiness that you seek to obtain through long detours, you can have it right away . . . that is, if you abandon the entire past, if you entrust the future to providence, and if you govern the present in accordance with piety and justice."[121]

A rule of life, then, but also "deep wisdom," which is the child's wisdom of which the "Marienbad Elegy" speaks, in a passage in which Goethe's spokesperson is Ulrike von Levetzow, the young woman whom he loves but will have to renounce:

> Hour by hour,
> Life is kindly to us.
> Yesterday has taught us little,
> To know the morrow is forbidden . . .
> Therefore, do as I do. With joyful understanding,
> Look the instant in the eye! Do not delay!
> Greet it quickly with lively benevolence
> Whether for action, for joy or for love
> Wherever you are, be everything, always childlike.
> If you are everything, you are invincible.[122]

Here again, concentration on the instant ("Look it in the eye!") corresponds to liberation from the past and the future, and to an attitude of greeting, acceptance, and consent with regard to being-in-the-world, which one lives in the instant. Here, what was the "health of the moment" of the ancients becomes the wisdom of children, that is, a spontaneous disposition to live in the present and greet it joyfully, without reflecting or seeking to understand. As Goethe said: "A child likes cake, without knowing anything about the baker, and a starling likes cherries, without thinking about how they have grown."[123]

"You have spoken well," he answers the girl, "for God has granted you the favor of the instant, and when he is by your holy side, each person feels, that for an instant he is fate's favorite. But the hint that I must leave you terrifies me. What good does it do me to learn such lofty wisdom?"[124]

The girl, who is still, in a way, in the world of childhood, lives spontaneously in the present instant. To look at her is to receive the grace of an instant, accorded by fate, which fills the soul with a spontaneous joy. The girl herself invites the poet to greet all of life in the same way, to extend this experience to each instant, and to look each instant in the eye. Yet the intensity of his grief at separation no longer allows him to practice this lofty wisdom.

However, a bit more than two months after writing the "Elegy," Goethe advised Eckermann, in one of his conversations, to practice that "lofty wisdom" that had always been his, in the deepest recesses of himself: "Hold fast to the present. Every circumstance, every instant is of infinite value, for it is the representative of an entire eternity."[125]

We can see here that for the person who "holds fast to the present," every instant is significant and full of meaning. Alongside the exceptional instant offered by fate, there is therefore room, in Goethe, for concentrating one's attention on the present instant, which can give meaning and value to any instant. Already in the course of his journey to Italy, on October 27, 1787, he considered that all intelligent people admit that "the moment [*Moment*] is everything, and that the excellence of a rational human being consists in conducting himself in such a way that his life, insofar as it depends on him, contains the greatest possible volume of rational, happy moments."[126]

To concentrate on the present moment means both to accept what destiny offers us at each instant and to interiorize it (*er-innern*), in order to tend toward a higher perfection. By concentrating on the present moment, consciousness, far from withdrawing, raises itself up to a higher viewpoint, from which one sees, as it were, the past and the future in the present, and it opens itself up to the infinity and eternity of being. For in attention to the present, the thought of the past and of the future is set aside only insofar as mulling over one's past defeats or fearing future difficulties gives rise to distraction, worry, hope, or, on the contrary, despair, which divert one from the attention one should pay to the present.

Yet the present itself, or rather "presence" (*Gegenwart*), when one pays attention to it, is not separated from the past and the future, insofar as it is linked to life, to the surging-forth of things, and the perpetual metamorphosis of reality. Let us recall what Goethe said about the dancer who, with a "beautiful agility . . . moves from one figure to another . . . so that we see the past, present, and future at the same time, and this is enough to transport us to a supraterrestrial state."[127] It is this past and this future that the artist's gaze grasps in the instant she chooses. Thus, there are privileged instants in which one perceives the permanence of the past in the present. Even in the "present" of the happiness of the meeting between Faust and Helen, past and present are closely linked to the present instant: Faust brings Helen back to her origins, Arcadia, and we glimpse the future birth of Euphorion. Goethe was always particularly sensitive to the presence of the past in the present. In *Poetry and Truth*, for instance, he alludes to the impression he had often had of seeing the past and the present united within a single reality, for instance in front of the cathedral of Cologne, which, he says, lends the present a strange, somehow ghostly air.[128] With regard to the funerary steles he saw at Verona, he writes, "The immediate 'presence' of these stones was extremely moving to me,"[129] both because these monuments have a moving "presence," and because they are a part of the past in the midst of the present.

Let us now return to the declaration made to Eckermann, which we mentioned above:

Hold fast to the present. Every circumstance, every instant is of infinite value, for it is the representative of an entire eternity.

Goethe often alludes to this relation between the instant and eternity, for instance in a letter to Auguste von Bernstoff: "If the eternal remains present to us at every instant, we do not suffer from the fleetingness of time."[130] Or again, in this concatenation of verses from the poem entitled "Vermächtnis" (Legacy): "Let reason be present wherever life rejoices in life."[131] This point at which life rejoices in life is precisely the present instant. "Then," the poem continues, "the past is enduring, the future is alive in advance, the instant is eternity." In the *Divan*, Suleika speaks as follows:

The mirror tells me: I am fair!
You say: growing old is also my fate
Before God, all must stand eternally
Love Him in me, for this instant of the gaze [*Augen-blick*].[132]

If one places oneself, so to speak, in the viewpoint of God—that is, for Goethe, of Nature—of what makes eternal becoming be born, the beauty of an instant is eternal, insofar as it is a moment of that eternal becoming. To love Suleika's beauty is to love, in an instant, the beauty of Being.

One might say that each instant is a "symbol" of Being, if one recalls that Goethe has described the symbol as the "living, instantaneous revelation of the unexplorable."[133] The notion of the "unexplorable" corresponds to what Goethe considers as the ineffable mystery that is at the basis of Nature and of all reality. It is its very fleetingness, its perishable character that makes the instant a symbol of eternity—"all that is perishable is merely a likeness"[134]—because this fleetingness reveals cosmic becoming, the eternal metamorphosis that is, at the same time, the eternal presence of being: "The eternal pursues its course through all things. Hold fast to being, joyfully."[135] Each instant passes and announces what comes to us. It offers a possibility of new creation, in the becoming of the self and the becoming of the world. Like life, it is ceaselessly destruction and creation, that is, ever-renewed novelty, ad infinitum. The divinity's intention, says Goethe in *Poetry and Truth*, is that, on the one hand, we should constitute our self (*verselbsten*) and individualize ourselves, and, on the other, that we should not fail, in regular pulsations, to strip ourselves of our self (*entselbstigen*), to de-individualize ourselves.[136] Sometimes, this theme takes on a mystic resonance in Goethe: "To find oneself in the infinite, the individual willingly accepts to disappear . . . to abandon oneself is a pleasure."[137] This is also the meaning of the famous poem "Selige Sehnsucht" (Blessed Nostalgia): "I wish to praise the living being that longs for death in the flame . . . / Until you have understood this Die and Become!, / You are but a gloomy guest on the dark earth."[138]

The ultimate meaning of Goethe's attitude toward the present is, then, by means of concentration on the present, and on the existence that we reach only in the instant, the happiness and duty of existing in the cosmos, a deep feeling of participation and identification with a reality that transcends the limits of the individual:

> Great is the joy of being-there [*Freude des Daseins*],
> Greater still is the joy one feels in existence itself [*Freude am Dasein*].[139]

Here, we reach the summit of the consciousness of existing.

Yet Goethe does not forget another aspect of concentration on the present. At each instant, one must strive to accomplish what the day demands of us, according to Goethe's expression (*die Forderung des Tages*): that is, to do one's duty in the present moment.[140] For Goethe, there is something sacred about this application to present duty. In the *Divan*, for instance, the poor old Parsi, an adept of the ancient Persian religion, persecuted by the Muslims, begins the testament he bequeaths to his coreligionists:

> And now, here is my sacred legacy
> Which I confide to my brothers' will and memory:

The hard observation of daily duties
There is no need for any other revelation.[141]

This means that genuine religion consists in this attention, at every instant, to accomplish one's daily duty, one's earthly task.

There are, we shall conclude, two different but related aspects to the notion of the present instant in Goethe: on the one hand, the exceptional instant, the unexpected opportunity offered by fate; and, on the other, the daily instants, to which, like the ancient philosophers, we can grant infinite value by foreseeing in their "presence" the course of eternal becoming and the eternal renewal of being.

The View from Above
and the Cosmic Journey

The Instant and the View from Above

We have said that certain exceptional instants could be achieved by the contemplation of nature. Goethe alludes to one of these instants in his essay "On Granite," written in 1784.[1] To understand this text, we must recall that for Goethe, granite represents the origin of the entire mineral kingdom. Thus, contact with granite is contact with the original earth:

> Sitting on a bare, lofty summit, looking out over a vast region, I can say to myself: "Here, you are resting immediately on a ground that reaches as far as the deepest places of the earth . . . Nothing is interposed between you and the solid ground of the originary world" . . . In this instant, in which the inner attractive and moving forces of the earth act upon me as it were immediately, in which the influences of the heavens hover more closely around me, I become attuned to higher considerations about nature . . . Here, on the most ancient, eternal altar, built immediately on the depths of creation, I offer a sacrifice to the Being of beings: I feel the first and most solid beginnings of our existence, I look at the world from above, these valleys, more steep or more gently sloping, and their distant, fertile meadows. My soul is

elevated above itself and above everything, and it longs for the nearby heaven.

A pregnant moment, that is in relation with all of cosmic becoming, all of cosmogenesis. In the instant in which Goethe sees the rocky formations, he simultaneously sees the long process that has given rise to them. It may be interesting to note that a few years previously, in 1779, Saussure, while climbing the Cramont in the range of Mount Blanc, saw the movement of the earth and of the sea that gives it birth, as he contemplated the mountain range.[2] Goethe then experiences a feeling of communion, with both the earth and the sky, which in him is always translated by the soul's movement of elevation above itself. Religious metaphors serve to describe what is, in a sense, a cosmic ecstasy: the granite rock is depicted as an altar[3] on which Goethe offers a sacrifice that is nothing other than the view from above, cast upon both the visible world and its beauty, and, in imagination, on its genesis.

We have already encountered this intimate link between the instant and the view from above with regard to the gestures of the ancient dancer who, in the instant, allowed us to glimpse past, present, and future and placed us in a supraterrestrial state. This can be explained by the fact that the view from above (*Blick von oben*) allows one to see a vast totality in a single glance (*Augenblick*), hence, in an instant. This is just as true for the poet as for the scholar, as we shall have occasion to repeat.

The theme of the view from above will thus often recur, richly ornamented, in Goethe. To understand it, however, we must, as in the case of concentration on the present, resituate it within the perspective of the ancient and Western tradition.

The View from Above in Antiquity: Peaks and Flight of the Imagination

Hans Blumenberg,[4] following Jacob Burckhardt,[5] affirmed that human beings of antiquity and the Middle Ages felt a genuine inhibition with regard to viewing the world from above, or imagining it as seen from above by human beings. According to them, this taboo was the result of the sacred nature of mountain peaks, and of primitive mankind's fear of them. In antiquity, the natural dwelling place of human beings was below, and the natural direction of the gaze was from below to above, since they were naturally "contemplators of the heavens." Thus, when Petrarch climbed Mount Ventoux on April 26, 1336, this should be considered a radical turning point in the history of the human spirit and a genuine conquest. This event revealed the intrepid nature of modern mankind,[6] while maintaining the trace of ancient mankind's interiority in the commentary Petrarch devoted to it.

Unfortunately, this affirmation is completely arbitrary. In this context, one cannot warn too strongly against the simplifications of historical psychology, which tends to want to identify decisive moments and turning points in the history of collective psychology. It is astonishing to see all the blindnesses, if one may say so, that historians attribute to the Greeks. They are said to have been unaware of linear time and of progress, and, as Jacques Le Goff thinks, they did not give much importance to the opposition between above and below:

> In the system of orientation of symbolic space, whereas Greco-Roman Antiquity had accorded a pre-eminent place to the opposition right-left, Christianity, while conserving an important value for this antinomic couple (at God's right hand), had privileged the above-below system from an early date.[7]

The texts we shall enumerate will, I believe, clearly show the inexactitude of such affirmations. Far from being taboo, the view from above was a vital necessity. Ancient people sought out mountain peaks and elevated points for their usefulness in daily life and their strategic importance. In the Homeric poems, we often read of the watchtower (*skopiê*), which allows one to see things from a distance. Thus, Homer evokes the goatherd who, from the height of his watchtower, sees a cloud that comes from the sea, pushed on by the Zephyr, which makes him decide to bring in his flock.[8] Thus, he alludes to the watchman who, from an elevated point, observes the surface of the sea, when, speaking of the horses of Hera, he makes this comparison:

> As far as into the hazing distance a man can see with
> his eyes, who sits in his eyrie gazing on the wine-blue water,
> as far as this is the stride of the gods' proud neighing horses.[9]

We can easily see that this is no matter of poetic imagination, but of everyday experiences: those of a goatherd or a watchman.

In the field of literature, from the Homeric poems until the end of antiquity, one finds no trace of the taboo to which, according to Burckhardt and Blumenberg, the view from above was subject. Quite the contrary: we often find the description of grandiose scenes provided by the view from above. In the third century BCE, Apollonius of Rhodes describes Jason's ascent of Mount Dindymon and the panorama he contemplates from this summit:

> Before their eyes appeared the Macrian heights and the entire
> coast of Thrace opposite, as if they held them in their hands. The
> misty mouth of the Bosporus and the hills of Mysia also appeared,
> and, on the other side, the stream of the Aesepus river and the city
> and Nepeian plain of Adrasteia.[10]

One gets the feeling that the poet is recounting an experience that is almost habitual. From the heights of a mountain, one sees the observatories and watchtowers of other people. The poet knows that from the top of a mountain, one gets the impression of seeing distant objects close at hand, but that they can also appear through the mist. The description is, moreover, limited to enumerating the geographical landmarks and their names.[11] Yet we are unquestionably in the presence of a view from above, which is of the same nature as that of Homer. As for Aristophanes, he makes the chorus of *The Clouds* sing as follows:

> Clouds everlasting, let us arise, revealing our dewy bright form, from deep roaring father Ocean onto high mountain peaks with tresses of trees, whence to behold heights[12] of distant vantage, and holy earth whose crops we water, and divine rivers' rushing, and the sea crashing with deep thunder. For the ether's tireless eye is ablaze with gleaming rays. So let us shake off the rainy haze from our deathless shape and survey the land, with far-seeing eye.[13]

In everyday life, seeking out high points and climbing mountains were routine, especially at the end of the Hellenistic period and the Roman era. We then find increasingly numerous testimonies to the importance people attached to the view from above. Villas were built on elevated sites so that their inhabitants could take in vast horizons at a glance: we have the testimonies of Seneca, the poet Martial, the author Pliny the Younger, and the poet Statius on this subject, and this fad was continued until the Byzantine period, as we can see from some poems of the *Palatine Anthology*.[14]

According to Burckhardt and Blumenberg, ancient people did not climb mountains, except, at most, in order to build temples there. Here too, however, we have formal testimonies that prove the contrary. First of all, in the first century CE, Seneca asks Lucilius to climb Etna, in order to make some observations concerning physics.[15] This ascent of Etna was also carried out at the beginning of the second century by the emperor Hadrian; in 125 to be exact. The *Historia Augusta* tells us that he climbed Etna in order to see the sunrise, which, it was said, appears as multicolored as a rainbow.[16] It was also in order to see the sunrise that he climbed Mount Kasios, near Ephesus, in 129.[17] According to the historian Ammianus Marcellinus, writing at the end of the fourth century CE, this was also a tradition at Antioch. He writes of the emperor Julian:

Finally, on a previously appointed festal day, he ascended Mount Casius, a wooded mountain rising on high with a rounded contour, from which at the second cock-crow the sun is first seen to rise. And as he was offering sacrifice to Jove, he suddenly caught sight of a man lying flat upon the ground . . .[18]

For Lucilius, for Hadrian, and for Julian, these climbs were neither touristic curiosities nor physical exercise. They were exercises that were at the same time philosophical and religious: the practice of physics and of the contemplation of the world.

I have spoken of famous ascents. Yet some texts allow us to glimpse that such explorations were frequently made. For instance, Lucretius tells of some observations made during climbs:

For the very facts and our own feelings when we ascend high mountains make it clear that the open spaces above are full of wind.[19]

Lucretius knows that there are many signs of lightning strikes on mountaintops. He has had occasion to use echoes to call out to his companions who became lost during one of these ascents, and he has heard it said that on the summit of Mount Ida, one sees scattered lights at daybreak that then gather together into a kind of single globe and form a perfect disk. Diodorus Siculus also describes this phenomenon in the first century BCE.[20] All these examples thus show that there was no need to wait for the fourteenth century and Petrarch's ascent to the summit of Mount Ventoux for people to dare to look at the earth and the sky from a mountaintop.

Yet one could also look at the earth from above by flying or floating; or at least one could imagine doing so. Such an aerial journey seemed to be reserved for the gods. Thus, Apollonius describes the flight of Eros toward the earth:

He traversed the fruit-filled orchard of mighty Zeus and then passed through the ethereal gates of Olympus. From there a path descends from heaven; and two peaks of lofty mountains uphold the sky, the highest points on earth, where the risen sun grows red with its first rays. And beneath him at times appeared life-sustaining earth and cities of men and divine streams of rivers, and then at other times mountain peaks, while all around was the sea as he travelled through the vast sky.[21]

As A.-J. Festugière remarked, a note by a scholiast in the margin of the manuscript indicates that Apollonius is imitating the way in which the poet Ibycus, in the sixth century BCE, evoked the rape of Ganymede, who was carried away to Olympus by Zeus's eagle.[22] We still have, moreover, a verse from this poem by Ibycus: "He flies over an abyss that is foreign to him,"[23] which lets us assume that the poet was trying to describe the strangeness of the experience of flying through space.

However, couldn't human technology conquer this privilege, which was common to the gods and the birds? It was imagined that in a mythical Crete, the ingenious technician Daedalus had fled, together with his son Icarus, from the labyrinth in which he had been confined, by constructing and using artificial wings. He had thus been able to land in Sicily, but Icarus, who, in his youthful audacity, had come too close to the sun, fell into the sea, because the heat had melted the wax that held together the feathers of his wings.[24]

The Philosophical Meaning of the View from Above among Ancient Philosophers

For ancient philosophers, the view from above was an exercise of the imagination by which one visualized seeing things from an elevated point, which one had reached by rising above the earth, most often by means of a mental flight through the cosmos. There is a very abundant ancient literature on this metaphor of the flight of the mind.[25] From the perspective we are now concerned with, I will mention only the texts that refer to a gaze directed toward the earth or toward the cosmos, or to a movement toward the infinite. One can observe that the imaginary movement of elevation on high is inspired by the desire to plunge into the totality, and even beyond the totality, into the infinite. In the words of the author of the treatise *On the Sublime*:

> The whole universe is not enough to satisfy the contemplation and thought of human beings; our concepts often pass beyond the limits that confine us.[26]

Thus, the view from above corresponds to a tearing away that frees one from terrestrial heaviness. However, this does not exclude a critical vision of the puniness and ridiculousness of what impassions most human beings.

When sketching the portrait of a philosopher in the *Theaetetus* (173e), Plato writes:

> It is only his body that is situated in the city, and resides in it. But his thought, which considers all things down here below as small and nothingness, holds them in no esteem and flies everywhere; measuring what is, as Pindar says, "beneath the earth," and its surface, and contemplating the stars "above the heaven," and everywhere examining the entire nature of each being, not lowering it to anything of what is close by.

In the *Republic* (6.486a), Plato again writes with regard to philosophy:

> Such a soul must not conceal any baseness, since petty-mindedness is incompatible with a soul that must always tend to embrace the totality and universality of the divine and the human . . . But the soul to which the elevation of thought and the contemplation of the totality of time and of being belong, do you think it holds human life in great esteem? . . . such a man will therefore not consider death as something to be feared.

Here, we can easily recognize the representation of a flight above earthly things, but we do not find a detailed description of a spiritual exercise of the view from above in Plato.

However, such descriptions do appear in the Platonic tradition. To be sure, in *Scipio's Dream*, Cicero presents this as something experienced in a dream.[27] Yet the author and his reader nevertheless turn it into a spiritual exercise, the former by writing the account of that dream, the latter by reading it. This exercise consists in imagining the vision of the heavens, the stars, and the earth that one can have from the heights of the Milky Way. What one's gaze embraces in such a case is the entire universe: the nine spheres, the outermost one of which is God himself, the stars, the planets, and finally the earth, with its mountains, rivers, and ocean. In such an experience, the individual tries to resituate herself within the Whole; one might say that this is a lived, internalized physics. It makes the soul understand the pettiness of human affairs, the vanity of glory, and the true meaning of the destiny of human beings, who are called upon to live not on earth but in the immensity of the cosmos.

Around the time of the Christian era, Philo of Alexandria evokes his philosophical experience:

> [I] seemed always to be borne aloft into the heights with a soul possessed by some God-sent inspiration, a fellow-traveler with the sun and moon and the whole heaven and universe. Ah, then I gazed down from the upper air, and straining the mind's eye beheld, as from some observatory [*skopia*], the multitudinous world-wide spectacles of earthly things, and blessed my lot in that I had escaped by main force from the calamities of mortal life.[28]

This time, it is through infinite space that the mind's flight takes off for the Epicureans. For them, the world we see is merely one of the worlds that extend throughout infinite time and space. In Cicero, for instance, an Epicurean evokes

the measureless and boundless extent of space that stretches in
every direction, into which, when the mind projects and propels
itself, it journeys onward far and wide without ever sighting any
margin or ultimate point where it can stop.[29]

Lucretius says of Epicurus:

forth he marched far beyond the flaming walls of the world, as he
traversed the immeasurable universe in thought and imagination.

And with regard to the quest for knowledge:

For, since the sum of space is infinite abroad beyond the walls
of the world, the mind seeks to understand what is there in the
distance, whither the intelligence continually desires to look forth,
and whither the mind's projection flies free of itself.

Or, again:

The walls of the world open out, I see action going on throughout
the infinite void.

Before recalling the infinity of the totality of things and the puniness of what surrounds us—the heavens, the earth—compared to
this infinity, Lucretius warns his reader:

This is where you must bring a gaze that goes far and sees from
on high, and you must look far into the distance and in every
direction.[30]

For the Epicureans, then, there is pleasure in plunging into the
infinite, or that which is without limit.

The flight of thought and the view from above also extend toward
the infinite among the Stoics, as Seneca attests: "Tell me rather how

closely in accord with nature it is to extend one's mind into the infinite!"[31] And Marcus Aurelius: "The soul extends into the infinity of Time."[32] Among the Stoics, however, there is only one finite universe, while infinity pertains to time, within which the same universe ends up infinitely repeating itself.

One could say that for the Platonists, Epicureans, and Stoics, the view from above is a kind of practice or exercise of physics, insofar as, with the help of knowledge about nature, the individual situates herself as a part of the Whole of the world, or the infinity of worlds. This vision provides joy and peace of mind. Epicurus affirms that we would have no need of the study of nature if we were not troubled by the fear of the gods and of death.[33] As Seneca says,

> The mind possesses, in its complete, full form, the good which human existence can achieve when it spurns all evil, reaches the lofty and the deep, and enters the innermost secrets of nature. Then . . . the mind wanders among the very stars . . .[34]

The view from above can also become a pitiless gaze brought to bear upon the pettiness and ridiculousness of what inspires man's passions; for from the perspective of the view from above, the earth is no more than a point as compared to the immensity of the universe or universes. "The earth seemed so small to me," says Scipio, as he recounts his dream in Cicero, "that I was ashamed of our Roman Empire."[35] This theme of the critique of human passions, when observed from a higher viewpoint, is broadly orchestrated in all the schools and especially, as we shall see, among the Cynics. It was not exempt from a certain contempt for the common man. Thus, Pythagoras, who appears at the end of Ovid's *Metamorphoses*, declares:

> It is a delight to take one's way along the starry firmament and, leaving the earth and its dull regions behind, to ride on the clouds, to take stand on stout Atlas' shoulders and see far below men

wandering aimlessly, devoid of reason, anxious and in fear of death.[36]

We find the same contemptuous gaze in Lucretius:

But nothing is more delightful than to possess lofty sanctuaries serene, well fortified by the teachings of the wise, whence you may look down upon others and behold them all astray, wandering here and there and seeking the path of life.[37]

In Seneca's *Natural Questions*, the soul of the philosopher, from high up in the sky, becomes aware of how small the earth is, of the ridiculousness of artificial luxury, and of the absurdity of wars fought to defend minuscule borders, and he compares human armies to troops of ants.[38] In Marcus Aurelius, our theme takes on a particularly realistic form:

For those who wish to talk about human beings should observe things on earth as if looking down from some place high above: herds, armies, farmers; weddings, divorces, births, deaths; the hubbub of the courts; deserted places; the diverse customs of barbarous peoples; celebrations, lamentations; marketplaces: the hodgepodge, and what is put together out of contraries . . . Look from above at the herds by the thousands, thousands of initiatory ceremonies, all kinds of navigations in stormy weather and calm, various things that come into being, come together, and depart . . . Bear in mind that if you were suddenly raised into the air, and contemplated human things and apprehended their variety, you would consider them negligible when you saw, at the same time, how many aerial and ethereal beings well around them.[39]

This effort to look at things from above thus enables us to contemplate the whole of human reality, in all its geographical and social aspects, as a kind of anonymous swarm, and to resituate it within the cosmic immensity. Seen from the perspective of universal nature, the things that do not depend on us, the things that the Stoics call "indifferents"—for instance health, glory, wealth—are brought back to their true proportions.

It is not impossible that these texts by Marcus Aurelius were influenced by models from the Cynic tradition. One can observe a certain analogy between the description he offers of the earth as seen from above and the vision of the human world evoked, in the context of imaginary cosmic journeys, by his contemporary Lucian, who was very much influenced by Cynicism. In his dialogue entitled *Icaromenippus or The Man Who Rose above the Clouds*, Lucian has the Cynic Menippus recount how he decided to go explore the heavens, to see things as they are, instead of contenting himself with the disappointing theories of the philosophers.[40] He therefore dons wings in order to fly—the right wing of an eagle and the left wing of a vulture—and soars off toward the moon. When he gets there, he sees the entire earth from above, and, as he says, like Homer's Zeus, he observes, now the land of the Thracians, now the country of the Mysians, and even, if he wishes, Greece, Persia, and India, which, he says, fills him with a variegated pleasure.[41] He also observes human beings: "the life of man in its entirety disclosed itself to me, and not only the nations and cities but the people themselves as clear as could be, the traders, the soldiers, the farmers, the litigants." Yet he also has the power to discover what goes on under the roofs, under the shelter of which each person thinks she is well hidden. After a long enumeration of the crimes and adulteries he thus sees being committed, Menippus sums up his impressions, speaking of a hodgepodge, cacophony, and a ridiculous spectacle: people quarrel over the limits of a nation, although the earth seems minuscule to him when seen from above. Their parcels of land, he says, are no bigger than the atoms of Epicurus, and the gatherings of people resemble swarms of ants. Menippus continues his journey through the stars to reach Zeus, where he derides the contradictory and ridiculous prayers that human beings address to him. In another dialogue, entitled *Charon* or *The Watchers*, the ferrymen of the dead—that is, Charon–asks for a day off to go up to the surface of the earth, to see what that life on earth could be that people miss so much when they arrive in Hell. This time, it is not a cosmic journey, but in order to better observe people, that he and Hermes pile several mountains on top of one another, as the Giants who wanted to scale the heavens had done.[42] We then find the same kind of description as in the *Icaromenippus* and in Marcus Aurelius: navigations, armies at war, trials, people working the fields, manifold activities, but always a life full of torments. "If, from the beginning," says Charon, "men realized that they are mortal, and that after a brief stay in life, they must leave it behind like a dream and leave everything behind on this earth, they would live more wisely and would die with fewer regrets." Yet human beings are unconscious: "They are like the bubbles produced by a stream, which disappear no sooner than they form."

The Greek subtitle of the dialogue entitled *Charon* is *Episkopountes*, "Those who keep watch." Cynic philosophers considered that their role was to keep watch over the actions of human beings, and they were like spies who lay in wait for the mistakes of human beings and denounced them. In Lucian's *Dialogues of the Dead*, Hermes ironically invites the Cynic Menippus to take his place beside the helmsman, so that he can keep watch over the others from a high position.[43] The words *episkopos* and *kataskopos*, "watchman" and "spy," are attested in the ancient tradition to designate the Cynics.[44] For them, this view from above was intended to denounce the senseless character of the way human beings live.

It is not indifferent, moreover, that it is Charon, ferryman of the dead, who, in the work named after him, looks at human affairs from above in this way. He sees things from the perspective of death. The Cynic denounces the madness of human beings, who, forgetful of death, become passionately attached to things, such as luxury and power, which they will inexorably be forced to abandon. This is why he calls upon people to reject superficial desires, social conventions, and artificial civilization, which are a source for them of trouble, concerns, and suffering, and he urges them to return to a simply and purely natural life.

Let us add that for Lucian, as we learn in his little book *How One Should Write History*, the view from above upon human affairs is not only that of a philosopher, but also that of a historian. More precisely, the historian's gaze must be that of a philosopher, that is, courageous, impartial, alien to any country, benevolent to all, giving nothing either to hatred or to friendship.[45] This attitude must be reflected in her way of narrating the facts. The historian, Lucian tells us, must be like Homer's Zeus, who casts his gaze now on the land of the Thracians, now on that of the Mysians.[46] Once again, we find this divine Homeric gaze directed toward the earth from above. This time, however, it is in order to find in it a model for the impartiality that must be expressed in the very structure of the narrative, thanks to the elevated viewpoint at which the historian situates herself. Here, the vision from above appears as the precondition for the historian's objectivity and impartiality. This is what the moderns were to call "the viewpoint of Sirius."[47]

The Medieval and Modern Tradition

The theme of the view from above, capable of changing the way we represent to ourselves our earthly existence, and hence, our way of living, was not to be found again until Pascal and Voltaire. Before them, what interests authors is primarily the curiosities of an imaginary cosmic journey. In the Middle Ages, the framework of the cosmic journey served above all to set forth the structure of the universe as the ancients pictured it to themselves. One of the first works of this kind was the *Cosmography* by Bernard Silvester, a remarkable member of the Platonic school of Chartres in the twelfth century.[48] As Hélène Tuzet has pointed out, there is no real journey in Dante's *Divine Comedy*: although Dante rises toward the Empyrean with Beatrice through the nine celestial spheres, "he traverses the sky without looking at it," and "the abyss of space does not exist for him."[49] He moves from one sphere to another instantaneously.

We encounter this literary genre once again at the beginning of the seventeenth century, first of all with the dream (*Somnium*) of Kepler, written in 1604 and published in 1634, which tells of a trip to the moon, and then with the *Iter exstaticum* by the famous Jesuit priest Athanasius Kircher, published in 1656, which describes a journey into the depths of the heavens. We also find it in *The Other World*, a trip to the moon and sun as told by Cyrano de Bergerac, published in 1657 and again in 1662.[50]

In the same period, however, the ancient theme of the contrast between the immensity of the cosmos and the puniness of the earth reappears in Pascal:

> Let man therefore contemplate all of nature in its lofty, full majesty, let him remove his gaze from the base objects that surround him . . . let the earth appear to him as a point as compared to the vast revolution described by this star [the sun], and let him be amazed at the fact that this vast revolution itself is but a most delicate point as compared to the one embraced by the stars that rotate in the firmament . . . All this visible world is merely an imperceptible stroke in the ample heart of nature.

Like the ancients, Pascal draws the conclusion that mankind must learn to evaluate the earth, kingdoms, towns, and himself at their proper value.

We also find in Pascal the theme of the infinity of time and space that we encountered in Marcus Aurelius:

> When I consider the short duration of my life, absorbed within the preceding and subsequent eternity, the small space I occupy, and even the one I see, lost in the infinite immensity of the spaces that are unaware of me and of which I am unaware, I am afraid,

and amazed to see myself here instead of there, for there is no
reason why here instead of there, why now rather than then.

It is interesting to see how this representation of the world's
immensity and the infinity of space, which brought serenity and
peace of mind to Epicurus, Lucretius, or Marcus Aurelius, brings
terror to a man of modern times, as in the famous exclamation: "The
eternal silence of these infinite spaces frightens me."[51]

In the eighteenth century, by contrast, there is a return instead
to the Cynic and Skeptic tradition of Lucian, with *The Devil upon
Two Sticks* by Lesage, who makes the roofs of houses transparent
in order to provide a better view of human vices, and with the
novels of Voltaire. His *Micromégas*, written around 1750, tells the
story of the eponymous character who lives on a planet close to
Sirius. Micromégas is gigantic in size, measuring eight leagues tall.[52]
Together with an inhabitant of Saturn, who is only one thousand
toises tall,[53] he undertakes a journey through the cosmos and winds
up on earth.[54] This, of course, is the opportunity for Voltaire to insist
on the puniness and pettiness of human beings and of the things of
the earth. However, it is not only Lucian's witty eloquence that is
revived; we also find in Voltaire the tradition of the cosmic journey
that elevates the soul:

> Zadig set out toward the stars. The constellation of Orion and the
> brilliant star of Sirius guided him toward the pole of Canopus. He
> admired those vast globes of light that look like faint sparks to our
> eyes, while the earth, which is in fact no more than an impercep-
> tible point within nature, seems to be something so grand and
> so noble to our greed. He then imagined men as they really are:
> insects devouring each other on a tiny atom of mud. This true
> image seemed to annihilate his misfortunes by reminding him of
> the nullity of his existence and that of Babylon. His soul darted
> into the infinite and, detached from its senses, contemplated the
> immutable order of the universe. Later, however, when he had

returned to himself and penetrated into his heart once more, he thought that Astarte was perhaps dead because of him, the universe disappeared in his view, and in all of nature he saw nothing but Astarte dying and Zadig hapless. As he was surrendering himself to this ebb and flow of sublime philosophy and overwhelming pain, he advanced toward the borders of Egypt.[55]

Zadig travels on earth, guiding his route by observing the stars. When he looks at the heavens, however, he is somehow transported there in his imagination. In a kind of ecstasy, he contemplates the order of the universe and feels himself swept into the infinite, which provides him, at least temporarily, with peace of mind.

At the end of the eighteenth century, André Chénier had the project of becoming a new Lucretius, as it were, by writing a poem entitled "Hermes," which was to describe the system of the earth, then the animal and vegetal species, then the birth and evolution of human civilization, and finally its final happiness in universal peace. The various drafts of this poem extend over a period from 1780 to 1792.

> Often my flight, armed with the wing of Buffon,
> Traverses, with Lucretius, to Newton's flame,
> The blue belt o'er the extended globe.
> I see being and life and their unknown source,
> In the rivers of aether, all the rolling worlds.
> I follow the comet with sparkling mane,
> The stars and their weight, their forms, their distances.
> I travel with them in their immense circles
> . . .
> The diverse elements, their hatred, their love,
> Their causes, the infinite, open up to my avid eyes.
> Soon, coming back down to our humid mud,
> I bring it verses aflame with nature
> Kindled by the pure rays of the Gods in my flight.[56]

Here we glimpse what was to be one of Goethe's basic ideas: the identity between the approach of the poet and the observer of nature, both of whom must maintain themselves above things in order to achieve a unique gaze upon the All.

The Various Forms of the View from Above in Goethe

For Goethe, the exercise of the view from above takes the form of a description of the impressions he experiences, either on the occasion of a real or fictional stay on a mountain summit, or during an ascent into the air, imagined after the model of a flight in a hot-air balloon, or in the course of a flight in the cosmos. A few years previously, the first human flight through the air had taken place, when the Montgolfier brothers had made their ascent on June 5, 1783. Goethe had been greatly impressed by this event, and he had followed with passionate interest all the similar experiments that had taken place in Germany at the time.[57]

Mountaintops and Experiences of Renewal

For Goethe, mountaintops were like magical places that have an influence on the people who reach them. As Wilhelm Emrich points out, it is typical of Goethe's old age to situate on a high mountain the decisive moment when a profound transformation takes place in his heroes, when they detach themselves from their past, in order to be rejuvenated, as it were, and orient themselves toward a new life.[58] This is probably because the view from above elevates the soul above daily life, making it see earthly life in an unaccustomed aspect. At the end of the third act of the *Second Faust*, after the death of Euphorion, Helen abandons Faust, leaving only her clothing (*Kleid*) in his hand, and Mephistopheles says to him: "This clothing will raise you above all that is common, into the ethereal space."[59] The item of clothing is then transformed into a cloud, which lifts Faust into the air. By flying, with the help of this cloud, he finds himself alone on the summit of a tall mountain at the beginning of the fourth act. Then, he is not content to "contemplate the deepest of solitudes beneath his feet," but he becomes aware of the meaning of his past and envisages a new future.

The essential part of his past appears to Faust in the form of two clouds, one in the form of Helen, the other shaped like Marguerite, which rise ever higher in the sky. The former "dazzlingly reflects the deep meaning of days gone by," while the latter reminds him of "the love of his dawn" and, as it rises into the ether, "takes with it the best part of him."

His future is a complete reorientation of life: to carry out an active life in the service of other human beings. During his flight which led him to the lofty mountain, he has seen the sea invading the land. He can then explain to Mephistopheles his great project of allowing an entire people to live sheltered from this threat. The realization of this plan will be described in the fifth act, in which the ambiguity and dangers of human action will appear.

Similarly, at the very beginning of *Wilhelm Meister's Journeyman Years*, Goethe also places his hero atop a mountain: "In the shadow of a powerful rock, Wilhelm was sitting in a terrible, imposing place, where the steep mountain path rounded a corner and quickly headed toward the depths."[60] As for Faust, so for Wilhelm, the mountain will be the locus and cause of the new orientation of his life. The profound change that takes place is not defined at the beginning of the chapter but expressed in a letter which, in this first chapter, Wilhelm writes to Natalie:

> Here I am at last on the summits of these mountains, which separate us by a barrier that is more powerful than the entire extent of the country already traversed.[61]

Thus, the high mountain signifies separation from the past, but also a new perspective that will ultimately have the same orientation as that of Faust: to devote himself to thought and action. In the case of Faust, however, this will be realized by letting himself be swept along by limitless ambition, while in the case of Wilhelm, it will be by being a "renunciant," as the novel's subtitle indicates, that is, being aware of his limitations, whether in the field of knowledge or in that of action. In both cases, Geneviève Bianquis speaks of "conversion to the social," rightly showing the importance of this orientation: "to transform the soul and life of human beings by acting on the material conditions of their existence."[62] Faust undertakes large-scale drainage works, while Wilhelm accompanies a group of emigrants to America as a doctor. As Geneviève Bianquis implies, it is not impossible that the model of Voltaire, who had devoted himself intensely to the development of agriculture, industry, and hygiene, to improving the life of the inhabitants of his fief of Ferney, may have influenced this interest on the part of the aging Goethe in works of social utility. As we shall see later with regard to the Genius floating above the terrestrial globe, the view from above cast upon nature can inspire a desire to act in the service of human beings.[63]

Mountaintops and Cosmic Experience

Already in his youth, mountaintops brought the poet a kind of revelation: it suffices to recall the stanza from the poem "To the Coachman Chronos" (1774). The stagecoach, whose itinerary represents life, is led by a coachman whom Goethe identifies with Time. It reaches a climax:

> Broad, high, magnificent, the gaze
> Plunges into life around it,
> From peak to peak,
> Soars the eternal spirit,
> Sensing eternal life.[64]

In the *Journeyman Years*, visiting mountain peaks is not only the occasion for a break and a reorientation, but ultimately, as in the text

on granite that we mentioned above, a kind of cosmic experience.
For instance, when, in the third chapter, Wilhelm meets his friend
Jarno, once again on a steep cliff, he is overcome by dizziness. Jarno
then makes the following remark:

> Nothing is more natural than feeling dizzy at the sight of an
> immense landscape before which we suddenly find ourselves, to
> feel at the same time our puniness and our grandeur.[65]

For Kant, becoming aware of the puniness and grandeur of
human beings is precisely the effect produced by the sublime, for
the infinite overwhelms us, but the thought of the infinite elevates
us, so that the feeling of the sublime is simultaneously pain, fear, and
pleasure.[66] It is probably in this perspective that Jarno adds: "There
is only true enjoyment when we must begin by feeling dizzy." This
is no longer a physical dizziness, but dizziness in the face of what is
inconceivable. As Erich Trunz remarks in his commentary on *The
Years of Travel*, "the gaze one casts upon the world from a mountaintop is, at the same time, the recognition of the infinite outside
us, and of the inner limits that are imposed upon our knowledge."[67]
For the person who is able to become aware of the sublime character
of what she sees, the view from above makes her go beyond what is
graspable and conceivable, placing her in the presence of what is infinite and inconceivable. This is what Wilhelm implies when he says:
"Most people remain in this state [that is, in a superficial vision of
things] throughout their lives, and never reach that splendid time in
which what is conceivable seems to us common and foolish."[68] Jarno
answers Wilhelm: "One may indeed call it a splendid time, for it is
an intermediary state between despair and adoration." Only superior
natures are aware of the limits of our knowledge of Nature. They
see what Goethe calls the originary phenomena, which one cannot
go beyond, and which, without expressing it, allow us to glimpse
what is inconceivable, ineffable, and absolute. Thus, they are situated
between the despair of not being able to explain the inconceivable,

and adoration before the mystery: one must "leave the originary phenomena alone, in their eternal peace and splendor."[69]

Flights of Birds, Balloons, and Poetry

If, as we have said, Goethe was so interested in the first balloon flights, it is because he dreamed intensely of freeing himself from weight, and of soaring like a bird, beyond all barriers, in his impulse toward the infinite. It is no accident if, in the first stanza of "Winter Journey in the Harz," the poem is compared to the flight of a vulture soaring above the clouds.[70] For Werther, it is the crane that symbolizes desires for flight:

How often have I longed, with the wings of a crane that flew above my head, to fly to the unlimited sea, to drink from the foaming cup of infinity that swelling joy of life.[71]

This is how the novel's hero evokes the paradisiac vision he once had of Nature and the state of mind he was in when, from the top of a rock, he contemplated the swarming of universal life. Faust echoes him when, contemplating a landscape illuminated by the setting sun, he imagines having wings that allow him to follow the sun in its course. He regrets that this is only a dream and that the wings of the body are not added to the wings of the mind:

And yet it is inborn in each
That her feelings press onward and upward
When, above us, lost in the blue space,
The lark sings its warbling song;
When, over the steep tops of the spruce,
The eagle soars on outspread wings;
When, over fields and seas,
the crane makes its way home.[72]

Let us pause for a moment to consider the particular nature of the emotion that the lark's song brings about in us. How could one fail to mention here the fine pages that Gaston Bachelard devoted to the theme of the lark in literature, for instance in Shelley, Meredith, and D'Annunzio? He cites this happy formulation that Lucien Wolff uses with regard to Meredith: "The lark moves . . . what is most pure within us." As Bachelard says, this time commenting on Shelley, "it actualizes and projects the joy of the universe."[73] For us, the lark is simultaneously the flight and the song that tear us away from terrestrial heaviness.

It is therefore not surprising that for Wilhelm Meister in the *Years of Apprenticeship,* the bird is the symbol of the poet, since "a poet, like a bird, can soar above the world." Detached from sordid interests and the worries of common mortals, the poet, when she looks at things on high, sees reality as it is: "Inborn in the soil of her heart, the beautiful flower of wisdom grows forth."[74] This, moreover, as Wilhelm affirms, is why he cannot practice a trade like other people.

For centuries, human beings have dreamed of flying like a bird, but they could do so only in imagination. However, on June 5, 1783, the dream became a reality. A human being actually tore himself away from earthly heaviness, and for Goethe, the balloon became the symbol of poetry. On May 12, 1798, Goethe wrote to Schiller:

> Your letter found me in the *Iliad,* as you desired. I always return to it, all the more readily in that one is always elevated above everything earthly, as in a balloon, and really finds oneself in that intermediary space in which the gods floated hither and thither.[75]

If Homer's poetry elevates us above the earth, it is because it makes us see the events it narrates, and the entire world, with the eyes of the gods, who, from the heights of the air and the mountains, contemplate the battles and sufferings of human beings, without, moreover, depriving themselves of the possibility of intervening at times in favor of one camp or another. This view from above of the Homeric gods fascinated Goethe. For instance, indulging in his passion for skating, he compares himself to Homer's Hermes, "flying over the sterile sea and the infinite earth."[76]

For Goethe, Homeric poetry is an example of "true poetry," which he defines as follows:

> True poetry announces itself by the fact that, like a secular gospel, it is able, through inner cheerfulness and external pleasure, to liberate us from the earthly burdens that weigh upon us. Like an air balloon, it raises us, along with the ballast that clings to us, into higher regions, and makes the confusing maze of the earth lie unfolded before our gaze, from a bird's-eye perspective.[77]

The last sentence alludes to the flight of Daedalus, who had fashioned wings for himself to escape the labyrinth in which Minos had enclosed him. For Goethe, the balloon pilot who tears himself from earthly weight, and Daedalus flying out of the labyrinth, symbolize the inner liberation and serenity that true poetry brings us. This tearing away from weight is found once again in the destiny of Euphorion, child of Faust and Helen, who is the incarnation of poetry, which, moreover, as Goethe implies, is personified by the figure of Lord Byron. Euphorion leaps, jumps, and finally rises higher and higher into the air, until, unfortunately, like Icarus, he falls and dies.[78]

Goethe speaks here of a "secular gospel." The expression is quite strong: poetry is thus "good news" for humanity. This definition of true poetry takes its place within a context in which Goethe criticizes English poetry, which he reproaches for inspiring a "gloomy disgust with life." On the contrary, true poetry must bring with it both pleasure and serenity. It frees us from terrestrial labyrinths. In Goethe's enthusiasm for Homeric poetry, which is "true poetry," we may glimpse the same idyllic representation of the ancient world as the one we observed in the context of the Goethean conception of the instant.[79] Yet we must recognize, above all, that the liberation brought about by true poetry is realized because such poetry implies a view from above, which detaches us from terrestrial, egoistic preoccupations, to resituate our life in this world within the vast perspective of the All. As Manfred Wenzel has rightly noted: "The true poet does not proceed differently from the true observer of nature. Both must maintain themselves above things to be able to achieve a unique gaze upon the All."[80] The goal is to perceive totality and unity, and not, as most people do, merely the details. Here, we find all the meaning of physics, which was practiced as a spiritual exercise by ancient philosophers, and which brought serenity and peace of mind. True poetry is thus a "secular gospel" insofar as it is ultimately a revelation, the revelation of Nature:

> What can man gain in life that's more
> Than that God-Nature reveal itself to him?[81]

Lynceus or the Pure Contemplative

Lynceus is the watchman who looks down from the heights of the tower of Faust's castle. His name refers to the extraordinary visual capabilities of the pilot of the Argonauts. He appears in the third act of the *Second Faust*, where, bedazzled, he sings of Helen's beauty. In the fifth act, it is to the beauty of the world that, bedazzled once again, he addresses his praise:

> Born to see
> Charged with observing
> Sworn to the tower
> the world pleases me.
> I look into the distance,
> I see nearby
> The moon and the stars,
> The forest and the deer.

Thus in all things I see
The eternal adornment
And since it pleases me,
I also please myself.
My fortunate eyes:
Whate'er you have seen,
Be it as it will,
It was so lovely![82]

Here, the look from the top of the tower is directed at the heavens and toward the earth. It inspires amazement, first at the sight of the various wonders of nature: the stars, the forest, and animals, wonders that Goethe designates by the expression "universal adornment" (*Zier*), which, as Friedrich Scheithauer remarks, corresponds to the Greek term *kosmos*, meaning both "adornment" and "order."[83] This vision places a human being in harmony with the world, but also with him- or herself: Lynceus finds pleasure in himself, because he finds pleasure in the "eternal adornment." Ultimately, moreover, it is existence itself that fascinates Lynceus: "Whate'er you have seen, / Be it as it will, / It was so lovely!"

As in Lucian, however, the view from above reveals not only wonderful splendors. It also makes known to us the evil actions committed by humankind. No sooner has Lynceus finished his hymn to the beauty of the world than he immediately sets the record straight:

It is not for my own amusement
That I am here so highly placed.
What abominable terror
Threatens me from the dark world!

And he describes what he gradually sees: Mephistopheles setting fire to the small house of Philemon and Baucis. He is horrified by the misfortune that strikes the old couple. Nevertheless, he describes the spectacle in great detail: the tree trunks in flames, colored reddish purple. Nature is beautiful in all its manifestations, but it is unaware of good and evil. I believe, following Albert Schöne, that the end of Lynceus's hymn in honor of the universal "adornment,"

My fortunate eyes:
Whate'er you have seen,
Be it as it will,
It was so lovely!

alludes in advance to the vision of the fire.[84]

Lynceus's view from above is purely contemplative. Enclosed within his tower, he can only look on but cannot act. Yet be it as it will or as it may, the spectacle is beautiful. We shall have occasion to return to the possible relation between this attitude in the face of the world perceived in all its aspects and that of Nietzsche.[85]

"Genius Floating above the Terrestrial Globe": Contemplation and Action

An entirely different perspective is opened up for us by a poem with the surprising title "Genius Floating above the Terrestrial Globe," one hand pointing to what is above, and the other to what lies below. This poem is an explanation of and commentary on one of the eight emblematic paintings (figure 1) with which Goethe had his house decorated for the fiftieth jubilee of the reign of duke of Weimar in 1825. According to the explanation given in a circumstantial writing, published in the same year,[86] four of these emblems represented the various arts: poetry was imaged by an eagle holding a lyre; painting was recognizable by a paintbrush inscribed within a crown of laurel; sculpture[87] was represented by a genius unveiling the bust of nature; architecture was symbolized by a square, a compass, and a plumb-line. Among the other four, two relate to the protection granted to the arts by the grand duke of Weimar and to the peace provided by the political authorities. As for the painting representing an urn on

FIGURE 1. Christian Ermer, detail from *Hovering Genius*, engraving, from Johann Wolfgang von Goethe, *Weimars Jubelfest: am 3ten September 1825* (Weimar: Wilhelm Hoffman, 1825).

a carpet, it signified, according to the commentator, the possibility for art to give a kind of life and beauty to lifeless objects. Finally, the emblem we are discussing, with its Floating Genius, symbolized "the contemplation of and meditation on what is above and what is below." We might add that it also personifies the imagination, which enables the flight of the spirit. In the painting, we see the summit of the terrestrial globe and the heavens, in which clouds appear. In the sky floats a genius in the form of a young boy endowed with wings and pointing at the sky with one hand and with the other at the earth.

The motif of a being floating above the earth is probably inspired by the figures of Daedalus and Icarus, which can be seen in some emblem books, for instance in a collection by Anselme de Boot (figure 2),[88] or in an edition of Ovid's *Metamorphoses*, illustrated by Martin de Vos in 1607 (figure 3).[89] It is possible, as we shall see, that Goethe was thinking of the adventure of Daedalus and Icarus when he wrote his stanzas on the Floating Genius:

> Between above and below
> I float toward the cheerful sight.
> I take delight in what is motley,

I refresh myself in the blue.
And when, in the daytime, the distance
Of blue mountains[90] ardently attracts me,
At night, the profusion of stars
Glows, splendid, above my head:
Every day and every night
Thus I praise the lot of mankind:
If he always thinks of what is Right,
He is always beautiful and great.[91]

A few years later, Goethe wrote another stanza, which may help
to understand the third one:

When, in the daytime, zenith and distance
Flow, blue, into the immeasurable,
When, at night, the supremacy of the stars
Closes the heavenly vaults,
So in the green, so in what is motley,
A pure mind fortifies itself.
And what is above, like what is below,
Benefits the noble spirit.

FIGURE 2. Anselmus de
Boot, *Daedalus and Icarus*,
from Jacob Typot, *Symbola
varia diversorum principum,
archiducum, ducum, com-
itum & marchionum totius
Italiae* (Prague, 1603).

FIGURE 3. Crispijn van de Passe, *Daedalus and Icarus*, engraving, from Ovid, *Metamorphoses* (1602–7). Courtesy of Rijksmuseum Amsterdam.

In the first stanza, the Genius that personifies contemplative imagination, amazed and dazzled by the splendor of the spectacle of the colors of heaven and earth, expresses itself in a way similar to that of Lynceus. In the following stanzas, however, the perspective opens up to the infinite. The genius describes the sublime, grandiose spectacle of the starry sky and the earthly mountains, which is a far cry from the limited horizons within which human beings are usually confined. As Karl Vietor remarks, it is no accident that Goethe insists on the blue color of the mountains and the azure sky.[92] For in his *Treatise on Color*, blue is, one might say, the color of the infinite, of that which is always beyond; it is a mysterious color. "This color has a strange and almost inexpressible effect on the eye," "an attractive nothingness," the color that always escapes us. "Just as we see the depths of the sky and the distant mountains as blue, so a blue surface also seems to recede before us."[93] The following paragraph explains this assertion: "Just as we willingly pursue a pleasant object that flees us, so we like to look at blue, not because it forces itself upon us, but because it carries us along after it." Blue attracts us because we usually perceive it in connection with an inaccessible depth into which we would like to plunge. "Zenith and distance / Flow, blue, into the immeasurable," says the poem's last stanza, in which it is not the Genius who speaks, but the poet himself, who in turn describes the experience of flying between heaven and earth. In this stanza, green and a multitude of colors are added to blue, thus echoing the wonder that the Genius expresses in the first stanza. Here in Goethe, then, the view from above is joined by the contemplation of all the colors in the world: that is, according to the *Treatise on Color*, the various mixtures of light and darkness. How could we fail to evoke the grandiose conclusion of Faust's monologue at the beginning of the *Second Faust*? The hero is awaiting daybreak in a mountainous landscape. When the star appears, however, his eyes cannot bear the light, and Faust turns away toward the waterfall, in which the light is reflected in a multicolored rainbow: "It is in a colored reflection that we have life."[94]

The flight of the Genius floating above the terrestrial globe also has an ethical dimension:

Every day and every night
Thus I praise the lot of mankind:
If he always thinks of what is Right,
He is always beautiful and great.

I have capitalized "Right" to indicate that Goethe did not intend to state a banal moral formula of the type: mankind finds his greatness in doing what is good and right (*das Rechte*). Yet the entire context suggests that this moral nobility is closely linked to what the Genius is contemplating: colors, sky, and mountains, above and below. Like Karl Vietor, I think that the expression *ins Rechte* designates the order and legality of the world, in which humankind must insert itself, thinking of itself in its right place within that order which is manifested by luminous phenomena, but also in the starry sky and in the laws of nature. This attitude has a twofold aspect. On the one hand, the view from above upon the multicolored world makes us become aware of a world to which most people pay no attention: the grandiose, sublime spectacle of the earth and the starry vault, of the cosmos of which we are a part. This brings about an elevation of our consciousness, especially if, as was the case for Goethe, this "colored reflection in which we have life" gives us a foretaste of the unbearable splendor of God-Nature. On the other hand—and this is essential for the Goethe of the final years—this "Right," within which humankind must situate itself, must be rediscovered in action in the service of the human community.

We can observe an analogous movement in *Wilhelm Meister's Journeyman Years*, when Wilhelm looks at the starry sky from the heights of a tower:

> The brightest night, shining and sparkling with all its stars, surrounded the spectator, who thought he was seeing the high vault of the heavens in all its splendor, for the first time.[95]

It seems to Wilhelm that he is contemplating the sky for the first time, first of all because clouds, roofs, and forests usually hide this spectacle from us, and one must rise above the earth to be able to enjoy it, but especially because a spiritual ascent is required to experience its sublime character. One must go beyond "the innermost worries of our heart, which, more than mist and storms, bustle about in every direction to darken the entire universe in our eyes." One must first achieve inner serenity in order to be able to see the world.

Wilhelm feels crushed by the grandiose spectacle: "moved and astonished, he closed both eyes. The immensity ceases to be sublime; it transcends our faculty of understanding, it threatens to annihilate us. 'What am I compared with the All?'—he said to his spirit—'How can I . . . stand in the midst of it?' " Yet Wilhelm "solves the riddle" by using expressions that are completely parallel to those we find in our poem. The Genius praised mankind's destiny by saying, "If he always thinks of what is Right / He is always beautiful and great." Wilhelm says: "Can you even think of yourself in the midst of this eternally living order, if nothing stands out in you that moves continuously, rotating around a pure center?"

This center Wilhelm speaks of is nothing other than humankind's moral conscience. The poem "Vermächtnis" (Testament) spoke of the moral conscience as an internal sun. Thus, the vision of the beauty of the world awakens, as it were, the individual's moral responsibility toward other human beings. "Even if," Wilhelm continues, "it were hard for you to discover this center in your breast, you would recognize it by the beneficent, benevolent effect that emanates from it and attests its existence." Paradoxically, the sublime spectacle of the cosmos, which crushes us, invites us to become aware of the moral duty that imposes itself upon us at every instant.

It may be, moreover, that, consciously or unconsciously, the traditional notion of the flight of Daedalus and Icarus exerted an influence here. The Genius floats, pointing toward the sky with one hand and with the other toward the earth, that is, as it were, the two directions of mankind's nobility, the thought of the cosmos and action on earth. As he floats, he remains in his rightful place, without rising dangerously like Icarus, whose wings melted because, in his youthful ardor, he had come too close to the sun.[96]

This Genius floating above the terrestrial globe thus represents the technique, attitude, and spiritual practice of the view from above, which human beings must adopt if they want to think of themselves, that is, integrate themselves within the cosmos. To float in one's rightful place: one might say that there is no better commentary on this poem than the posthumous poem by Nietzsche entitled "Rules of Life," a title that seems, moreover, to echo Goethe's poem "Rule of Life," which we have discussed with regard to the instant.[97] In both cases, we glimpse the intention to propose an art of life:

To live life willingly
You must stand above it!

Therefore, learn to raise yourself up!
Therefore, learn—to look down!
. . . Don't stay at ground level!
Don't rise up too high!
See the world at its most beautiful
From halfway up the height![98]

In these *Journeyman Years*, devoted to human action in all its
forms—whether the subject is pedagogy, for instance, or a project
to emigrate to the United States—it is both very surprising and
very significant to find multiple allusions to exceptional states of
becoming aware of the ineffable and infinite nature of the cosmos,
which are accessible to only a few people. It is these experiences,
however, that, as it were, provide the basis for moral action and
care for other human beings. This close connection between cosmic
consciousness and moral consciousness appears in a surprising way,
for instance, in the strange figure of Macarie. She is able to mentally
travel in the cosmos and is like a star among the stars. She "seems
to have been created only to detach herself from what is terrestrial,"
and yet, throughout the book, one can observe her qualities as a
director of conscience, and the calming influence she has on all
those who surround her. More modestly, Wilhelm is crushed by
the sublime vision of the starry sky, but nevertheless remains a man
of action who practices the career of a surgeon. Aren't Macarie and
Wilhelm embodiments of that "noble spirit" that the poem on the
Floating Genius talks about, for whom the things above and the
things below—that is, the contemplation of the cosmos and action
on earth—provide equal enrichment? In this context, Erich Trunz
evokes the famous conclusion of Kant's *Critique of Practical Reason*:
"Two things fill the soul with ever-renewed admiration and venera-
tion: the starry sky above me and the moral law within me."[99] For
Goethe, cosmic consciousness and moral consciousness are closely
linked, for it is the spectacle of the laws of nature that invites the
soul to find within itself the duty of action in the service of others.

Ultimately, doesn't this Genius that floats between heaven and earth represent poetry, which, as Goethe used to say, tears us away from heaviness like a balloon? How does he differ from the eagle who, in the series of eight allegorical paintings, also floats between above and below, and who is, precisely, the symbol of poetry?[100] In the poem Goethe wrote about him, he reproaches him for singing too much of the things above and not enough of those below, of human beings on earth. From this perspective, it appears that for Goethe, the view from above and the sublime states can inspire, but cannot replace, moral action and the care for other human beings.

So far, I have not discussed the fourth stanza of the poem on the Floating Genius:

> *Memento mori*! Enough of that,
> I'd rather not repeat it;
> In the flight of life, why should I
> Torture you with its limits?
> Therefore, like an old curmudgeon,
> I recommend to you, *docendo*,
> My dear friend, in your own way,
> Just *vivere memento*![101]

By its peculiar tone, this stanza seems utterly foreign to the theme of the view from above of the Genius floating above the terrestrial globe. It makes fun of the Scholastic vocabulary and the somber monastic horizon, constantly confronted by death. However, several precise details ought to attract our attention. First of all, Goethe speaks of life as fleeting. In this perspective, the Genius is ultimately the living human being. Life is a flight situated between the celestial and the terrestrial, between the starry sky and the colors of the earth. The second detail: if life is a flight, it is a drive, an aspiration toward the infinite that must not be disturbed by the idea of an end and a limit. Here, Goethe is a disciple of Spinoza: "The Sage's meditation is not a meditation on death, but on life."[102] In this context, we can evoke a scene from the *Apprenticeship*, in which Wilhelm Meister, visiting the Room of the Past imagined by Natalie's uncle, sees, on a sarcophagus, a personage reading a scroll on which these words are written: *Gedenke zu leben* (Don't forget to live).[103] Here, we encounter once again Lynceus's "Yes" to life and the world, "It was so lovely!," or that of the poem "The Fiancé," "Whatever it may be, life is good."[104]

We have seen that the theme of the view from above in Goethe takes its place within a long, rich tradition. Yet we can also observe that Goethe's originality as compared with this tradition is considerable. The theme of the contempt for earthly things, illustrated by Voltaire and Lucian, has completely disappeared. Goethe does, of course, speak of humankind's puniness; but although they feel crushed by the spectacle of the cosmos, human beings rediscover all their dignity by inserting themselves within the universal order and the legality of nature. The view from above is above all a drive toward the infinite, but also a bedazzlement in the face of the world and life. As in antiquity, however, it is a spiritual exercise that demands that the person who practices it place herself in a certain moral disposition. The view from above opens up unsuspected perspectives upon the cosmos and human life, and brings about a kind of cosmic ecstasy. To accede to it, however, one must, like Wilhelm contemplating the stars, carry out a spiritual ascent, freeing oneself from material concerns and interests, in order to be capable of amazement and admiration and to perceive the sublime. It is possible that Kantian theories of the beautiful and the sublime had an influence on Goethe. One might say that for Kant, only a good soul is capable of feeling the beauty of nature, because such a soul is not blinded by egotistical interests.[105]

The View from Above after Goethe

During Goethe's lifetime, Leopardi mentioned the view from above with regard to the poet and the philosopher. In 1823, three years before Goethe wrote his "Genius Floating above the Terrestrial Globe," Leopardi noted in his journal, entitled *Zibaldone,* that inspiration and enthusiasm correspond to a kind of view from above:

> The lyric poet, in inspiration, the philosopher in the sublimity of speculation, the man of imagination and feelings in the time of his enthusiasm, any man under the spell of a strong passion, in the enthusiasm of tears, and, I even dare to say, fairly heated up by wine, sees and regards things as if from a height greater than that which the mind of human beings usually consists.[106]

Leopardi goes on to explain that this view from above allows one to see, all at once, a multitude of objects that one usually considers separate from one another. Here, we find an idea similar to that of Goethe, for whom one must remain above things in order to achieve a single gaze directed toward the All.

Almost fifty years after Leopardi, we find the theme once again in Baudelaire. At the beginning of *The Flowers of Evil,* four poems are devoted to the poet or to poetry: "Blessing," "The Albatross," "Elevation," and "Correspondences." In "The Albatross," the poet is compared to a bird made to soar, a "prince of the clouds," who is clumsy and ridiculous when he comes back down to earth. Yet the flight of the poet's mind is described in a great detail in "Elevation":

> Above the ponds, above the valleys,
> The mountains, woods, clouds, and seas,
> Beyond the sun, beyond the ethers,
> Beyond the confines of the starry spheres,
> O my spirit, you move with agility,
> And, like a good swimmer who delights in the waves,
> You gaily cross the deep immensity
> With ineffable, masculine pleasure.
> Fly far away from these morbid vapors;

Go purify yourself in the higher air,
And, like a pure, divine liquor,
Drink the bright fire that fills the limpid spaces.
Behind the boredoms and the vast sorrows
That load foggy existence with their weight
Happy is he who can, with vigorous wing,
Dart toward the luminous, serene fields,
He whose thoughts, like larks,
Fly off toward the heavens in the morning,
Who soars over life, and understands without effort
The language of flowers and silent things![107]

The flight of the mind carries him off beyond the terrestrial, and even beyond what is visible in the heavens. As we have seen in Goethe, here the poet tears himself away from earthly weight, cares, and material and carnal interests. He darts beyond the All, into the infinite. This flight provides a purification and a kind of intoxication, in which the soul drinks the celestial fire like liquor. The last stanzas oppose life on earth—morbid miasma, boredom, vast sorrows, foggy existence—to the medium into which the spirit launches itself: limpid spaces, luminous and serene fields. The spirit is compared to a lark flying off free toward the heavens.

The view from above and the flight of the mind are thus linked: the spirit "soars over life." The end of the poem is very significant. Why is it said that he who flies away toward the infinite in this way "understands without effort the language of flowers and silent things"? It is because the spirit has rediscovered its purity and its innocence by this purifying flight. It is not surprising that in the collection entitled *Flowers of Evil*, this poem is followed by "Correspondences," since the latter provides a kind of key for understanding this "language of flowers and silent things." In Baudelaire, then, we find once again what Goethe called "true poetry," which was at the same time detachment from terrestrial weights and contemplation of the mystery of Nature.

Baudelaire also feels this flight of the spirit when listening to the prelude of Richard Wagner's *Lohengrin*:

> I felt myself freed from the bonds of heaviness, and I rediscovered, in my memory, the extraordinary pleasure that circulates in high places . . . I then fully conceived of the idea of a soul moving in a luminous medium, an ecstasis made of pleasure and knowledge, and soaring above and far away from the natural world.[108]

Yet the theme of the view from above does not only appear from the perspective of poetry. It can also serve to define the spirit in which philosophers and historians look at terrestrial things. This is what is known as the "viewpoint of Sirius." The origin of the expression is probably to be found in Voltaire's *Micromégas*, since the eponymous protagonist, who is an inhabitant of Sirius, sees the things on earth in a way that could be called "the viewpoint of Sirius," although Voltaire does not use this expression. The same viewpoint can be found in a letter by Heinrich von Kleist, written in 1806, which expresses the despair of a person who becomes aware of the insignificance of his terrestrial life within the infinity of space: "What can be the name of that little star that one can see from Sirius when the sky is clear?"[109] I believe that the expression "viewpoint of Sirius" appears for the first time in Ernest Renan in 1880:

> When one places oneself in the viewpoint of the solar system, our revolutions scarcely have the amplitude of the movements of atoms. From the viewpoint of Sirius, it is even less.[110]

For years, the editorials by Hubert Beuve-Méry in the newspaper *Le Monde* appeared under the title "the Viewpoint of Sirius." To place oneself in the viewpoint of Sirius was to practice a spiritual exercise of detachment and distancing, to achieve impartiality, objectivity, and a critical spirit. It means resituating particular things within a universal, if not cosmic, perspective.

Ultimately, it is the gaze of a poet, a philosopher, and a historian that we find in Nietzsche, when he writes:

> Everything necessary, when seen from above and in the sense of a *great* economy, is also what is useful in itself. One must not merely bear it: one must *love* it . . . *Amor fati*, that is my innermost nature.[111]

Here, the view from above resituates an event within the perspective of the All and justifies a Yes to the world and to reality, even in its most atrocious aspects.

Aeronauts and Cosmonauts

What is utterly extraordinary in our era is that it has witnessed the realization of those cosmic journeys which, for thousands of years, had been either dreams, literary imaginations, or spiritual exercises. In a sense, one could say that Western humanity has long prepared itself spiritually for the actual cosmic voyage, and that it has tried to glimpse in advance the transformations that this voyage could entail for the consciousness of individuals and the idea that humanity has of itself and of the world. In particular, we have seen how the cosmic journey and the view from above, conceived as spiritual exercises, could lead some philosophers, such as Seneca, Marcus Aurelius, or Lucian, to denounce the vanity and the injustice of social inequality and the absurdity of war. We have seen how, thanks to these spiritual exercises, people could conceive of themselves as citizens of the cosmos, and how, as they practiced them, they had the feeling of a transfiguration and a transcendence of the human condition, which freed them from the fear of death and provided them with inner peace and serenity.

The view from above is not, moreover, achieved only by the imagination. We have seen the mountain-climbing practiced in antiquity by Hadrian and the Emperor Julian, and by Petrarch in the Renaissance. In Goethe's time, mankind began to tear itself away from earthly heaviness by means of the balloon. Then came aviation. Yet cosmic flights were an absolutely new experience. For the first time, human beings saw the Earth in its entirety from above, in a real vision. One can thus wonder whether the real experience brought about, in those who lived through it, inner states that were analogous to or completely different from those of the philosophers and poets, like Goethe and Baudelaire, who merely imagined it. The question is immense, and I will only be able to answer it imperfectly, for two reasons: first, from the perspective in which I have placed myself so far, I wish to take into account only people's relation with the Earth which they see from above, or with the cosmos in which they are immersed, but there are many other relations—social, physiological, technical—that would be foreign to my investigation and with which, moreover, I am incapable of dealing. Second, because my knowledge of the testimonies of astronauts talking about their inner states is very limited. I encountered this field of study about twenty years ago, but have not had the time to work on this question since then. I hope the reader will forgive me if I can only communicate my old reflections, based on the testimonies that were known at the time. I had been invited to participate in a conference entitled "Frontiers and Conquest of Space: Philosophy Put to the Test," which took place in Paris in January 1987.[112] The goal of the conference was to answer the question: will cosmic voyages bring about a mutation or a transformation in mankind? Along the same lines, the same year saw the publication of the collection of studies entitled *Spatiopithecus: Toward a Mutation of Mankind in Space.*[113] The following year, a collection of testimonies by astronauts illustrated by photographs appeared under the title *The Earth Viewed from Heaven.* These are the bases of my documentation.

Obviously, the state of weightlessness is essential for astronauts. Some have even spoken of *homo ingravitus.* However, this state has consequences that are much more complex than Goethe and

Baudelaire could have foreseen when they imagined a flight of the mind, soaring above the terrestrial sphere. For them, being torn away from terrestrial heaviness could only bring about a state of lightness and of liberation from the cares and turpitudes of life. Yet neither Goethe nor Baudelaire could have imagined the reality of this experience when it is lived through: its physiological dangers, the metamorphosis of bodily behavior, the fact of finding oneself in a medium where there is neither up nor down, and which is not vertically structured; the fact of finding oneself floating in the universe like the Earth itself, like one star among the stars in the cosmos.[114]

What, now, of the astronaut's relation to the Earth? Once again, this is a highly complex relation that preserves some aspects of the literary and philosophical tradition, but also introduces new elements. What disappears completely—and, moreover, had already disappeared in Goethe—is contempt for the Earth and its inhabitants. Of course, some astronauts admit that they are impressed by how small the Earth is in the cosmos: "I smile when I realize the ridiculous and relative immensity of our planet."[115] First of all, however, they are seduced by the beauty of the Earth, and, like Goethe, by the variety of its colors.[116] Above all, however, the Earth seen from the heavens awakens love and solicitude in them. In the words of the astronaut Wubo J. Ockels: "I think the fact of being in space, and being able to observe Mother Earth will gradually give birth to a protective feeling toward it."[117] It is remarkable that the expression "Mother Earth" recurs so often in the astronauts' testimonies. In this experience, however, human beings find themselves in an ambiguous situation. They feel themselves to be "of the Earth," but they are also freed from the Earth, and, to a certain extent, from the human condition.[118] As opposed to the terrestrial world, "I was part of the rest of the universe," as Michael Collins remarked.[119] One might think of a kind of "oceanic feeling" of communion with the All. "You can no longer understand how attached you were to that agitated matter beneath you," observed Thomas Stafford.[120] At the same time, the astronauts feel nostalgia for the Earth, the breeze and the smell of the Earth.[121] Yet the Earth appeared to the astronauts from a wholly different perspective, and, like the philosophers of antiquity, some of them denounce the absurdity of the borders that divide it: "The Earth: so beautiful, since the national borders have disappeared."[122]

Finally, there is the incommunicable nature of this experience. The "astronaut's syndrome," says Wubo Ockels, is precisely that she has lived through an incommunicable experience. The author is speaking about a meeting of astronauts in Budapest. They all meet, and know what they are talking about. "But the problem is as follows: every time an astronaut says: 'flying in space is wonderful, it's amazing, there are no borders. Why, then, if we are overwhelmed by this vision of the world, why don't we make peace, etc.?,' he is not taken seriously." "The fact that a handful of astronauts travel the earth crying 'How beautiful the world is!' won't change anything. So what? The only thing that could help would be if the politicians went there for real. They should get their own idea."[123]

The experience of the cosmic flight produces a profound transformation in those who experience it, as is attested by Edgar Mitchell, who, on the one hand, alludes to a new relation to human beings—"We went to the moon as technicians. We came back as humanitarians"—and, on the other, to a new relation to the universe: "I suddenly felt that the universe is intelligence, harmony, and love."[124]

It is hard to say whether all space travelers have such ideas. Perhaps not all of them are capable of carrying out the internal cosmic journey that philosophers, poets, and sages have dared to undertake, and which consists in freeing oneself internally from a way of seeing that is too partial or too anthropomorphic, in order to see all things from the perspective of the cosmos. Without an internal cosmic journey, without a view from above that is experienced as a spiritual exercise of detachment, liberation, and purification, space travelers will continue to take the Earth along with them into space: not the Earth that is a part of the cosmos, but the one that is a symbol of the human, all too human, the symbol of human pettiness. In that case, space risks being nothing more than the enlarged theater of those absurd wars of religion that continue to tear humanity apart in the early twenty-first century. The conquest of space runs the risk of merely providing a more vast field for human madness.

3

The Wings of Hope
The Urworte

It is once again a flight of the mind that takes us far from the Earth and even far from the constraints of fate that we encounter in the strange poem entitled *Urworte. Orphisch*: "Originary Words. In the Orphic Manner."[1]

DAIMÔN: DEMON[2]

As on the day that gave you to the world,
to greet the planets, in conformity with[3] the sun's position,
You developed straightway, and continued without cease,
Following the law by which you had begun.
You must be thus, you cannot escape yourself,
As Sibyls and Prophets had already said,[4]
And no time, no power can fragment
A Form, stamped with a seal, that develops as it lives.

TUKHÊ: THE COINCIDENTAL

Yet the strict limit is obligingly[5] bypassed
By a changing[6] being who changes with and around us.
You do not remain alone, but form yourself in society.

And you probably act as others do;
In the course of life, this falls now in one direction, now in the
     opposite one;[7]
It is a trinket, and we dawdle our way through it.
The circle of years has already gone round in silence,
The lamp awaits the flame to ignite it.

EROS: LOVE

It does not take long to appear: he hurtles down from the heavens
Where he had soared from ancient Chaos.[8]
He soars on airy feathers,
Around brows and hearts, throughout the springtime day;
Now seems to flee, returns from flight;
Then there is such well-being in suffering, so sweet and anxious;
Full many a heart dissolves in the universal,
Yet what is noblest devotes itself to the One!

ANANKÊ: CONSTRAINT

And thus, once again, it is as the stars wished:
Determination and law;[9] and all will
Is only willing just because we had to will;
And in the face of this will, our free choice keeps silent.
That which is most cherished is scolded from our heart.
Will and caprice resign themselves to the harsh "one must";
Thus, in the end, we merely seem to be free, for over many years,
We are more constricted than we were at the beginning!

ELPIS: HOPE

And yet, of this limit, this bronze wall
The most hateful gate bursts open
Though it stand with the ancient duration of rocks!
A being moves, light and unbridled
Above the ceiling of clouds, fog, and rainstorms,
It grants us wings and raises us up with it;

You know it well! It swarms through all the spaces![10]
One beat of its wings, and the eons[11] are behind us.

Daimôn, Tukhê

As K. Borinski showed in 1910,[12] Goethe was inspired for the titles
of these stanzas by reading Zoega's *Abhandlungen*, translated and
published by Fr. G. Welcker in Göttingen in 1817;[13] more specifically, by Zoega's dissertation contained in this collection, entitled
"ΑΓΑΘΗ ΤΥΧΗΙ. Tyche und Nemesis."

In this dissertation, after discussing the general notion of Tukhê
and its mythical depiction, Zoega noted that in antiquity, just as a
Tukhê was assigned to every place, every house, every family, and
every act of human life, so a Tukhê was attributed to each person,
which, united within her personal Daimôn, determined her destiny,
the difference being that Daimôn was related more to what was
internal, and Tukhê more to what was external.[14] In the Homeric
poems, the word "Daimôn" evokes individual destiny. A fragment
of Heraclitus affirms, in an ambiguous, obscure way, that "a human
being's particularity or character is her *daimôn*," without its being
possible to tell whether the Daimôn determines human individuality
or whether, on the contrary, the Daimôn is nothing other than the
individuality that characterizes each human being.[15] It must be admitted, moreover, that from Plato to Marcus Aurelius,[16] the Daimôn
appears as a reality which, at the same time, is ourselves and transcends us, which chooses us or which we choose. It is often conceived
as a kind of guardian angel, but one that personifies, as it were, the
individual's destiny.[17] In any case, the traditional notion is perfectly
epitomized in a fragment of Diagoras of Melos: "It is in accordance
with the Daimôn and Tukhê that all is accomplished for mortals."[18]
In the *Phaedo*, we read of the Daimôn "to whom each person, while
he lives, has been entrusted by fate."[19] In book 10 of the *Republic*, on
the subject of the destiny and the generation of souls, we find the
Daimôn and Tukhê together, but also Anankê, or Necessity: first in

the proclamation by one of the Moirai (Lachesis), addressed to the souls at the time of their incarnation: "You will choose your own Daimôn. The first one whom the lot has designated shall choose the first life, to which he shall be linked by Necessity (Anankê)."[20] Contrary to popular belief, it is the soul that chooses its character, or its Daimôn; but once this choice has been made, it is obliged by Anankê to submit to the consequences of its choice, that is, to live a specific kind of life. One can no longer free oneself from the individuality one has chosen and the destiny that is linked to that Daimôn, as Goethe says in the first stanza: "You must be thus, you cannot escape yourself!" Plato wants to absolve the gods of any responsibility for the evils that overwhelm humanity, whereas human beings accuse the divine powers when fate goes against them. This is the context in which Tukhê appears: he who, without reflecting, has chosen a tyrannical way of life, discovers too late the consequences of the choice of that life, and then wrongly accuses the demons and Tukhê.[21] In his commentary on this dialogue, Proclus specifies that the Daimôn presides primarily over what is within—that is, the movements of the soul—while Tukhê reigns primarily over external things, that is, over the relations between the individual and the world surrounding him.[22] In this same commentary by Proclus moreover, we find an even better formulation: "The daimôn carries out the soul's contract with the All, while Tukhê, in contrast, carries out the All's contract with the soul."[23] The Daimôn demands that the chosen type of life be fulfilled, while Tukhê attributes the circumstances linked to that type of life. With regard to a man who has failed in an attempted murder, the dialogue that Plato entitled *The Laws* declares that one must respect the Tukhê and the Daimôn of such a man, because Tukhê has not been completely negative, and the Daimôn has taken pity.[24]

Daimôn, Tukhê, Eros, Anankê, and Elpis

In Plato, the whole of human destiny was inscribed within a cosmological and astral context. Yet the various powers were not linked explicitly to a specific star. In the continuation of his dissertation, Zoega turns toward a strictly astrological aspect of this representation, beginning with the identification between Tukhê and the Moon, which can be explained because the Moon often changes shape. This relation "already" appears, he says, in the Orphic hymn to Tukhê. Zoega uses the expression "already" because he believed that the *Orphic Hymns* belonged to the ancient Orphic writings. Today, however, the consensus is that they were written during the second or third century of our era, for a religious community in Asia Minor,[25] so that this testimony is relatively late. In any case, the hymn to Tukhê does indeed identify it with Artemis, and hence with the Moon: "Tukhê who appeases, protectress of roads, Artemis who is Queen."[26] We should note in passing that the hymn following this one in the collection of the *Orphic Hymns* is addressed to the Daimôn.

Yet let us return to Zoega's text. To demonstrate the identity of Tukhê and the Moon, he then adduces a text by the Egyptian astrologer Nechepso, quoted by the astronomer-astrologer Vettius Valens in his *Anthologies*, written in the second century of our era. In fact, we do indeed find in Vettius Valens texts identifying Tukhê and Sêlênê (the Moon),[27] but since these texts do not explicitly attribute this identification to Nechepso, all we can say is that Vettius Valens's work claims to be based on Nechepso and Petosiris. These two personages were respectively an Egyptian priest and pharaoh, to whom an astrological treatise, written between 150 and 120 BCE, had been attributed apocryphally. Thus, this means that this identification of Tukhê with the Moon was known in the second century BCE. Zoega also mentions another astrological text that makes the same comparison: this time, it is a passage from the *Saturnalia* of Macrobius, written in the fifth century of our era, which also is based on the authority of the "Egyptians," who quite probably correspond to the Hermetic writings. It is all the more necessary to read it in that we will recognize in it the source of Goethe's poem, at the same time as it allows us to glimpse the poem's symbolic and emblematic background:

That, in Mercury, it is the Sun that they worship, is clear from the caduceus, which the Egyptians devoted to Mercury, fashioning it in the form of two snakes, male and female, united together. These two snakes are bound together in the middle part of their twisting bodies, by the kind of knot that is called "of Hercules." Their upper parts, curved into a circle, complete the area of a circle by their mouths joined in a kiss. Beneath the knot, their tails return to the hilt of the caduceus; and they are adorned by wings that sprout from the same point of the hilt. The Egyptians also extend the symbolism of the caduceus to the horoscope of human beings, which is called 'genesis.' They speak of the four gods who preside over the birth of a human being: Daimôn, Tukhê, Eros, and Anankê. The first two, they claim, signify the Sun and the Moon, for the sun is the source of the breath, heat and light, and the engenderer and guardian of human life, and for this reason, it is believed to be the Daimôn (that is, the god) of a human being when born. Tukhê is the Moon, because it is in charge of bodies, which are agitated by the vicissitudes of chance. Eros is represented by the kiss, and Anankê by the knot. We have already explained why the wings are added. The twisting bodies of snakes have been chosen primarily for this symbolism, because of the winding path of both celestial bodies.[28]

Here we recognize four of Goethe's originary words, which are thus situated within an astrological tradition that enumerates the powers that exert an influence on human destiny. At the same time, however, one sees, appearing behind this figure, the structure of the caduceus, which can serve to explain the structure of Goethe's poem.

As Zoega had remarked, popular traditions opposed the Daimôn, a power that imposes her destiny upon the individual, and Tukhê, a power which, by influencing external circumstances, comes to interfere with the Daimôn. In Plato, Daimôn, Tukhê, and Anankê do not seem to have any direct relation with a given star, and serve only to describe the component parts of human destiny, which, moreover, are linked to the general movement of the cosmos. Later, however, these elements were to be placed in relation to stars, which were thought to determine them. This is what we find in the text by Macrobius that we have just cited.

Macrobius, who wrote in the fifth century of our era, attributes to the Egyptians both the consecration of the caduceus to Mercury and the application of this symbol to the horoscope of human beings. Macrobius's text is part of a broader ensemble in which he is probably using treatises by the Neoplatonist Porphyry, in which this philosopher showed that all the gods can be identified with the Sun by their names or their attributes.[29] The passage that Macrobius devotes to the caduceus is intended to show that Hermes-Mercury is identical to the Sun. This may allow us to suppose that it was accepted that the Egyptians, to whom Porphyry is alluding (these may have been books of astrological Hermetism), established a relationship between, on the one hand, the caduceus and the course of the sun, and, on the other, between the caduceus and the planet Hermes. In fact, the caduceus was the symbol of Hermes in astrology. Macrobius is probably thinking of the Egyptian astrologers Nechepso and Petosiris when he affirms that for the Egyptians, the caduceus is the symbol of the horoscope.

In the *Panaretos*, which was attributed to Hermes Trismegistus and was cited by Paul of Alexandria,[30] an astrologer of the fourth century CE, we find, as Zoega remarks, an analogous but more developed system, in which the lots of human beings corresponded to the seven planets: Tukhê to the Moon, Daimôn to the Sun, Eros to Aphrodite, Anankê to Hermes, Tolmê to Ares, Nikê to Zeus, and Nemesis to Kronos. Whether the powers are seven or four in number, these lots were either points determined on the Zodiac, on the basis of the lot of Tukhê, which was determined as a function of the Sun and the Moon, or dice, which one threw on a table intended for this purpose.[31] In his *Commentary on Plato's Republic*, Proclus alludes to the calculation of the positions of the different lots:

What determines the Daimôn is the Sun; what determines Tukhê is the Moon. This is why the lots of the Daimôn and of Tukhê can be discovered in our nativities on the basis of these two [the Sun and the Moon], as is clearly known to those who are versed in astrology.[32]

Here, Proclus is alluding to the manner of calculating the lots of the Daimôn and of Tukhê from the position of the Sun and the Moon. The same word (*klêros*/κλῆρος) designates the lot which, according to Plato's dialogue, souls choose when they are incarnated,and the lot that is determined in astrology. As far as the astrological calculations are concerned, one can find, for instance, the points at which, in a given individual case, the four lots of the Daimôn, of Tukhê, of Eros, and of Anankê are located in two horoscopes published by Neugebauer and Van Hoesen.[33] Vettius Valens explains the various meanings that the lots of Tukhê, the Daimôn, Eros, and Anankê can assume, according to whether they are favorable or not.[34]

To these four powers, Goethe adds Elpis, or Hope. He had glimpsed it in Zoega's text, when this author showed that Anankê, whom Macrobius represented in the form of the serpents' knot in Hermes's caduceus, was, once again, none other than Tukhê, but conceived as the totality of the corporeal causes that determine events. In this regard, Zoega wrote:

All is subject to her [to Anankê] save the indomitable audacity of the human spirit, which we call, by another name, Hope, and also except for Victory, who consolidates the throne of Zeus.[35]

We will have occasion to return later on to this theme of Hope. One may wonder why Goethe gave his poem the subtitle "in the Orphic manner." Macrobius speaks only of the Egyptians and of Mercury, which, along with the allusions made by other authors to Nechepso and Petosiris, may entitle us to assume that these are

Hermetic astrological sources.[36] The five divinities who preside over human fate, according to the *Urworte*, do not belong to the Orphic tradition, except for Eros in his cosmogonic role, but to the mythology and philosophy that could be described as classical, which had been taken up in astrological speculations. Here, as K. Borinski rightly saw, the word "Orphic" would designate a literary genre rather than a religious or doctrinal tradition.[37] According to Borinski, Goethe had discovered it thanks to his reading of the *Mythological Letters* exchanged between Hermann and Creuzer at the time of the composition of the *Urworte*. It was the genre of "theological" poetry, as opposed to popular Homeric poetry. The word *Urworte* had been used by Hermann in this correspondence to designate sacred discourses (*hieroi logoi*): "philosophemes" originally presented in imagistic form, which became mystical doctrines by means of an esoteric interpretation.[38]

Human Destiny

It seems that what fascinated Goethe in Macrobius's text was what he called "a concentrated representation, conceived since the most distant Antiquity, of human destiny,"[39] such that the stanzas it inspired in him "open an infinite space to reflection, and allow us to see, as in thousands of mirrors, what we ourselves have experienced."[40]

In this text by Macrobius, it is, among other things, the mention of the horoscope that must have attracted Goethe's attention. We know, after all, how carefully the author of *Poetry and Truth* details, at the beginning of his work, the position of the planets at the moment of his birth:

> On August 28, 1749, while the clock struck noon, I came into the world in Frankfurt on the Main. The constellation was propitious. The Sun was in the sign of Virgo, and was at its culmination for that day. Jupiter and Venus gazed at it in a friendly way. Mercury was not hostile.[41]

As Charles Du Bos rightly noted, the first stanza of the *Urworte*, devoted to the *Daimôn*, seems to echo the opening pages of *Poetry and Truth*.[42] In both works, we find the Sun in its relation with the planets, and the state of the heavens at the moment of birth. Bettina Brentano, who heard this detail from Goethe's mother, told how in his childhood, Goethe "fixed his gaze toward the stars, which, it was told, presided over his birth."[43]

Goethe himself commented on the first four stanzas in a way that may shed light on them up to a point, but that sometimes seems quite banal and prosaic as compared to the mysterious conciseness of poetry. With the help of the stanzas themselves and of Goethe's commentary, we can glimpse that the poem states the laws that govern the destiny of human beings, and perhaps of all things. For it is remarkable that Goethe published this poem for the first time in the scientific journal *Zur Morphologie*, in 1820. Each in its own way, the four powers—Daimôn, Tukhê, Eros, and Anankê—determine and orient the course of an individual's life.

The first stanza is thus devoted to the Daimôn, that is, the first power that determines destiny. Goethe will return to the notion of the Daimôn in the commentary on the second stanza, evoking, in this context, the famous "demon" of Socrates, who "sometimes whispers in one's ear what should be done."[44] In fact, the Daimôn of the *Urworte* does not act intermittently, but, on the contrary, appears as internal necessity, which imposes upon the personal individuality its unique characteristic, produced and symbolized by the unique configuration of astral powers that presided over its birth. It is a force of growth that can unfold only if it remains faithful to its law of growth and remains within its proper limit. The individual is condemned to be herself: "You must be thus, you cannot escape yourself." These notions of limit and of law assume a value that is both central and ambiguous in the poem. They are felt to be the precondition both for existence and for development in harmony with nature, and as an obstacle to the individual's aspirations. This is why the second stanza, devoted to Tukhê, seems to open with a feeling of liberation: "Yet the strict limit is obligingly bypassed / By a changing being who changes with us and around us."

At first glance, Tukhê, Chance, or changing Fortune may seem to be a fortunate opportunity to escape ourselves and the strict limit which the Daimôn imposes upon us. This is why, in this regard, Goethe uses the adverb *gefällig*, which introduces a connotation of pleasure and satisfaction. To the rigorous law, Tukhê opposes chance, variety, and the unexpected, and this is pleasing to young people. Since early childhood, it represents the entire interplay of encounters with a specific environment, specific persons, specific events. One is shaped within society. Unfortunately, this confrontation with anyone and anything risks smothering the personality by plunging it into the world of banality, futility, vulgarity, and conformism: "And you probably act as others do." Here we encounter *das Gemeine* once again, "the common," "the vulgar," which, as we have seen,[45] Goethe views as the worst danger for human beings. In his commentary on the first stanza, Goethe had already described the pernicious effect that the encounter between the Daimôn and Tukhê can produce:

> To be sure, this solid, tough being [the Daimôn], who develops only out of itself, enters into all kinds of relations, whereby its initial, original character is inhibited in its effects and hindered in its inclinations, and our philosophy calls what then comes upon the scene Tukhê.[46]

Goethe forcefully expresses the same idea in *Poetry and Truth*. He begins by describing the near-perfection of young children: "If children continued to grow as they indicated, we would have nothing but geniuses."[47] Unfortunately, as a result of the encounter with things and human beings, matters will turn out quite differently. One is reminded of the famous regret of Saint-Exupéry, at the end of *Land of Men*: "What torments me . . . is, in a way, that there was a murdered Mozart in each of these men."[48] Among the dangers of accidental encounters, moreover, Goethe accorded an important place to repressive education. In a conversation with Eckermann, he sings the praises of the young Englishmen he meets at Weimar, "who have the courage to be what nature made them be," and who are treated, at home, with much more respect than are young people in Germany:

> Among us, everything tends to tame our dear youth at an early stage, to extirpate all nature, all originality, all wildness [*Wildheit*], so that at the end of the day, there is nothing left but a Philistine.[49]

With regard to this text, Charles Andler rightly points out that Goethe here anticipates the lamentations of Nietzsche, when he deplores the "philistine" spirit—that is, narrow-minded, trivial, and petit bourgeois—of the domesticated men, incurable mediocrities, produced by modern education and civilization.[50] From this viewpoint one might say that the Daimôn corresponds to a natural force of growth, which is, as it were, vegetal: "the typical form that unfolds as it lives." We know how much Goethe admired the workings of a living being: "how well-adapted it is to its state, how true it is, how existent."[51] This is a motion that goes from the inside to the outside. In contrast, Tukhê represents that movements that are external to us and do not depend on us: encounters with other people, but also the random nature of events, that game of chance we know as daily life. The twofold action of Daimôn and Tukhê is therefore decisive for an individual's fate. It is the encounter between innate factors and those that are accidental. "Daimôn and Tukhê," as Freud, who knew his Goethe well, was to say, "determine a man's fate."[52] This is what he calls the interaction between constitution and experience.

Youth takes pleasure in the games of Tukhê, in this movement now in one direction, now in another, which does not become fixed in anything and is not satisfied with anything. The encounter between Daimôn and Tukhê thus runs the risk of enclosing the individual within games and futility. Yet it can also cause a flame to shoot forth: that of Eros, the third power that determines the individual's fate.

> Here [in Love] the individual Daimôn and seductive Tukhê are united to one another; man only seems to obey himself, letting his own will reign, indulging his own impulses; and yet these are accidental occurrences that slip in, something that turns him away from his path.[53]

Here, Goethe certainly seems to be recalling Macrobius's description of the caduceus, in which Eros was represented by the kiss exchanged by the two snakes, that is, Sun and Moon, Daimôn and Tukhê.[54]

The Eros mentioned in this stanza is at the same time the "creative" Eros of which Orphic mythology speaks, "soaring from ancient Chaos," and the winged Love, son of Aphrodite in Hellenistic poetry, he who awakens desire in all beings in the spring. It is a force that dominates every being. This flying Love engenders fickle loves: it comes and goes, flees and returns. Here again, we encounter the movements in opposite directions of which Goethe spoke in the context of Tukhê. Once again, it is a game: this time not a futile one, but a mixture of pleasure and suffering, sweetness and anguish. The encounter between Daimôn and Tukhê that gives birth to Love is, in fact, a kind of trap for many human beings:

> He thinks he can grasp something and he is caught; he thinks he has won and is already lost. Here again, Tukhê plays her own game: she lures those who have lost their way into new labyrinths.[55]

We might thus be led to think, says Goethe, that "that which seemed to be designed for what is most particular dissipates and dissolves into the universal." In this dramatic play, most people lose their personality and their freedom, precisely because it is not their partner's personality to which they become attached, but only the pleasures of the senses, which, moreover, fade in multiplicity. "Yet," continues Goethe in the stanza devoted to Eros, "what is noblest devotes itself to the One!" The stanza thus ends on an almost triumphal note and with the representation of two personalities who freely choose each other. Nevertheless, the commentary Goethe provides to this stanza hints that things are much more complex:

> Yet it can happen that love completely transforms the Daemon, somehow taming this obstinate, egoistic force that finds it hard to put up with the obstacles that Tukhê places in its path.[56]

In that love which a person feels for the being which chance has made him meet, he may become aware of his freedom of choice. He can attach himself to the beloved being by an exclusive decision and transcend his egotism, thus showing that he is not "determined by Nature alone," and that he can "embrace another being like himself in an eternal, indestructible inclination." Here, we find the poem's triumphal tone once again.

However, the continuation of the commentary suggests that a new trap may perhaps lie hidden in this triumph of the Daimôn. For this free decision in fact has as its consequence the renunciation of freedom. One must live together: two souls in a single body, two bodies in a single soul, which then come to be joined by a child. This great body of the family suffers from illnesses, concerns, and worries: "All that amorous inclination allowed itself becomes a duty," which, moreover, is sanctioned by the ceremony of marriage. This, then, is an encomium of marriage, but a mitigated praise that refuses to conceal the "thousand duties" that will weigh upon the individual. And yet, as Goethe remarks, "this relation is as desirable as it is necessary, so that one accepts the drawbacks because of the advantages."[57] The end of the commentary on this stanza devoted to Eros thus expresses the bitterness of the individual who thought he was freely choosing and finds himself the prisoner of a "thousand duties." Some interpreters have deduced that the following stanza, dedicated to Anankê, expresses the disappointment of individual freedom in the face of the constraints and duties imposed by society.[58] The text of the stanza could imply this. We want, it says, only because we must. The "one must" leaves no room for spontaneity. What is most dear to us is brutally driven out of our hearts—one might think that this is because of social pressure. As we advance in life, we are more and more cramped for space, doubtless because of the obligations that weigh on us.

However, it seems to me that we must make a careful distinction between what Goethe says about the social constraints that weigh upon love and marriage in the commentary on the preceding stanza, and what he says in the following stanza about the pitiless, universal Necessity to which individuals are subject. In the commentary on the stanza on Eros, Goethe merely expresses an idea that is dear to him, and that we shall encounter once again in the poem "Amyntas": when one enjoys an advantage, one must accept the disadvantages that derive from it.[59] Every happiness has its price, which must be paid. As the uncle of the "beautiful soul" in *Wilhelm Meister's Apprenticeship* says, in a somewhat trivial way, with regard to the sacrifice we make to keep something that is dear to us: "one cannot have the money and the merchandise at the same time."[60] Or again, according to the *Maxims and Reflections*, "Voluntary dependence is the most beautiful situation; and how could it be possible without love?"[61] On the contrary, in the stanza dedicated to Anankê, we must not forget the first verse: "it is as the stars wished." The will of the stars represents the will of the All, that is, inescapable Fate or the will of a god, as *The Journey in the Harz in Winter* already put it forty years earlier:

For each,
A god has marked out his path
Beforehand.[62]

"Determination and law": such is the precondition for all existence. Human beings think they freely will, but they want what they want because they must want it, and they must want it because "the stars," that is, Fate, or the general order and course of Nature, have willed them to be so. They thought they were acting according to their will, but in fact it was decreed in advance, as a function of their Daimôn, that they would want what they thought they freely wanted. Thus defined, will (*Wille*), since it is predetermined, cannot leave any room for choice (*Willkür*), or individual spontaneity. For her part, the individual believes she does as she wishes, following her whims, but she does not know that in fact she is predestined, by the fact that she is and that she is such by virtue of her fate, to will precisely what she thinks she freely wills. In fact, as Goethe often repeats, human activity is subject to laws of bronze.[63]

Paradoxically, it may happen that this will, which the individual believes is personal but which is imposed upon her by her Daimôn and by Fate, is frustrated by that same Fate. This is the meaning of the verse: "Will and caprice resign themselves to the harsh 'one must.'" For instance, an individual has willed to become attached to a loved one, and has willed this because she had to, because her Daimôn destined her for that love; nevertheless, that love will be torn from her heart by Fate. Necessity apparently seems to oppose itself. This paradox can be compared to the one Goethe states in the twentieth book of *Poetry and Truth*, when he sets forth his ideas on the "demonic." He describes it as a power that manifests itself only through contradiction: it is nether divine nor human, neither demoniacal nor angelic, but it represents a phenomenon that cannot be explained by either intelligence or reason, a superhuman or semidivine power, a force that is creative but also destructive, seductive, almost irresistible, which exists in all of nature but is predominant in some men, such as Napoleon, for instance. "Nothing can defeat such people, unless it is the universe itself, with which they have joined battle."[64] E. Trunz thought, apparently correctly, that when Goethe speaks about "the universe," he is probably alluding to the Russian winter that vanquished Napoleon.[65] These demoniacal men, who are the instruments of Fate, are defeated by Fate.

Goethe continues: "And perhaps it is from this kind of observations that emerged the maxim—strange, but immensely important[66]— *Nemo contra deum nisi deus ipse.*" There has been much discussion about the origin and meaning of this maxim.[67] We need not enter into this controversy, but we do have to understand in what sense Goethe cites this formulation. At first glance, it means: only God can oppose God. Here, however, in the context of the "demoniacal," the word "God" means a semidivine power, and especially a power brought into existence by God, that is, by Nature or Fate. Only Fate itself can oppose a being whose will is imposed on it by Fate. The paradox thus consists in the fact that it is Fate itself that provokes what seems to oppose it. Already in 1782, the fragment on Nature, which is not by Goethe but was inspired by him, said: "One obeys her laws when one resists them; one also cooperates with her when one tries to act against her."[68]

Our quotation from *Poetry and Truth* gives us the occasion to discuss the relation that may exist in Goethe between the notion of the Daimôn and the notion of the "demoniacal," which is essential in his work. E. Trunz has quite aptly remarked that the Daimôn of the *Urworte* is proper to each human being, whereas the demoniacal is manifested only in exceptional beings.[69] Nevertheless, in Goethe's view, the Daimôn and the demoniacal have in common the fact that they are powers that dominate human beings, and that lead them, although they believe they are guiding themselves. Speaking, during a conversation with Eckermann, about great inventions, lofty inspirations, and great thoughts, which, he says, "are unexpected gifts the man receives from above," Goethe adds: "It is akin to the demoniacal, which, since it is overwhelming, does with man what it pleases, and to which man unconsciously abandons himself, while believing he is acting on his own initiative."[70] This is exactly the situation which, as we have seen, is described in the stanza devoted to Ananké: because of the inner necessity represented by the Daimôn, we want only because we must want, in conformity with the will of the stars, that is, of a higher power. The Daimôn of the *Urworte*, insofar as it determines and guides us, thus belongs ultimately to the vast domain of the demoniacal.

Whereas in this passage from the conversations with Eckermann, this higher influence is considered as a grace that inspires wonder, the stanza devoted to Anankê expresses, in a seemingly definitive, brutal way, the disappointment and disillusion that come to conclude all dissatisfactions that the soul, as Plato would say, or the individual has experienced upon discovering all the lots that determine her destiny. The Daimôn was a promise of harmonious growth for the newborn being. Yet it was also a predetermination and a predestination, which condemned her to be only what she was: "You cannot escape yourself." Tukhê was a promise of an encounter with other beings and an entire multitude of events, capable of introducing variety and fantasy into the growth of the individual; yet it risked smothering the personality in futility and conformism. Nevertheless, in the encounter with Love, Tukhê might offer the individual the possibility of opening up and transcending herself in another personality, and of choosing in this way, by a free decision, to unite with it in an unbreakable bond. Then, however, love became duty and obligation. Finally, the individual recognizes the absolute power of Anankê, Constraint or Necessity, to which she has been subject throughout her life. She has done everything "as the stars wished," as the first verses of the poem announced. "In the end," as the stanza on Anankê declares, "we merely seem to be free." Freedom and choice had been mere illusions. Once again, as early as 1771, more than forty years previously, Goethe had said in his speech for Shakespeare's birthday:

> His plays all revolve around that secret point (which, until now, no philosopher has seen or determined) at which the particularity or our ego, the putative freedom of our will, collides with the necessary course of the All.[71]

This problem was to haunt Goethe throughout his personal life, which he represents as subject to the "demonic," or higher powers, both in the course of events and in the successes of his artistic creation. It is significant that Goethe's autobiography, *Poetry and Truth*, begins by evoking the stars at his birth and ends with a passage from *Egmont*, the Goethean drama inspired by the idea of the "demonic," which suggests that the horses of Fate drag us along in a mad race, without our being masters of the starting point, the trajectory, or the point of arrival: at best, we can avoid some obstacles:

> As if spurred on by invisible spirits, the solar horses of time race along, taking with them the light chariot of our fate: all that remains to us is to hold the reins courageously, and to avert the wheels, now to the right, now to the left, here from a rock, there from a cliff. Where is it headed? Who knows? He barely remembers where he came from.[72]

The image is quite a powerful one, since one can imagine the anguish of a person being hauled along mercilessly by bolting horses.

We encounter this idea of the illusion of freedom once again in Schopenhauer, who cites the first stanza of the *Urworte* in his *Essay on Free Will*, to show that the necessity to which our actions are subject is based on the innate, individual character that Goethe presents as none other than the *Daimôn*. His exposition of the relations between will and necessity corresponds rather closely to what Goethe says in the stanza devoted to Anankê:

> A human being does at all times only what he wills, and yet does it necessarily. But that rests on the fact that he is what he wills: for from what he is, everything that he does at any time follows necessarily.[73]

In our poem, however, when despair reaches its culmination, a triumphal cry unexpectedly makes itself heard in the last stanza: the most hateful gate bursts open. An invincible force opposes Necessity and transcends it, escaping from the labyrinth in which

it was locked up: the mysterious Hope of the aging man and poet.
He found it, as we have said, in Zoega: "To Necessity, all is subject,
except the indomitable audacity of the human spirit, which we call,
by another name, Hope." Goethe was able to recognize its symbol
in the wings of Hermes's caduceus: "One beat of its wings, and the
eons are behind us!" Macrobius himself had related these wings
to the flight of thought.[74] Nevertheless, this figure "without weight
or constraint" is eminently Goethean. Curiously, however, Goethe,
who provided only a succinct, not very explanatory commentary on
the stanza on Ananké, referring to the reader's individual experience,
refuses to give any commentary on Hope:

> How joyfully do we therefore hasten to the last verses, on which
> every delicate soul shall willingly take charge of forming a com-
> mentary, from a moral and a religious viewpoint.[75]

For our part, we are in no hurry, and will return to this theme of
Hope only after a lengthy detour.

Autobiographical Aspects?

In his commentary on the stanza devoted to Ananké, Goethe appeals
to his readers' memories and personal experiences. One can therefore legitimately wonder whether the description of human fate provided by the *Urworte* also reflects events in his life. This question is
very hard to answer. Some indications allow us to suppose this, but
in view of the concise style of the poem and its enigmatic nature, we
cannot be sure. As we have seen, the mention of the constellation
that presides over birth and determines the Daimôn probably goes
back to a childhood memory. And when Goethe writes in the second stanza devoted to Tukhê: "You do not remain alone, but form
yourself in society," there may be an allusion to Goethe's youth, for
the first chapters of *Poetry and Truth* recount the complex relations
Goethe had with other children and adolescents: the mockeries he

underwent, the dubious affairs he became involved with as he frequented youths of "lower classes." This may explain the verse: "And you probably act as others do."

As opposed to the stability of the Daimôn, the notion of Tukhê introduced an element of mobility. The opposition between the solid and the moving in the perspective of human destiny already existed in Goethe's mind, well before he read Zoega's dissertation in 1817. In fact, Tukhê often appeared as a mobile power in emblem books—those collections of symbolic images, accompanied by moral maxims, that had great success since the Renaissance—some of which were present in Goethe's library. In 1777, he had erected in his garden at Weimar an altar dedicated to Agathê Tukhê, "Good Fortune" or "Smiling Fortune" (figure 4).[76] The monument, which was very simple, consisted of a cube on which a sphere rested. The sphere, which easily rolls, was traditionally the emblem of Tukhê: it signified mobility, inconstancy, and chance; while the cube represented solidity and constancy. In an emblem book from the seventeenth century, this motif of the sphere placed on top of a cube is accompanied by the legend: "That which was mobile becomes immobile" (figure 5).[77] The altar does indeed seem to symbolize Goethe's situation at the time. After several passionate, agitated years, he was transformed by the love he felt for Charlotte von Stein. Goethe's *Tukhê* led him to this encounter, and from this viewpoint it was a "Good Fortune." It came to be immobilized on the cube, which may represent virtue, or in any case, stability.

As far as Eros is concerned, Goethe had long known that he is "happiness in suffering," "sweetness in anguish." Yet are there precise allusions to Goethe's loves in the stanza devoted to Eros and in his commentary, and perhaps in the stanza devoted to Ananke as well? Three details may attract our attention. First, the verse "But what is noblest devotes itself to the One!"; then, in the commentary, the idea that free choice yields to duty; and finally, in the fourth stanza, the sad regret: "That which is most cherished is scolded from our heart." One could accept that when speaking of "the noblest," Goethe was thinking of himself. But when did Goethe really devote

FIGURE 4. Anonymous photo of Goethe's Altar of Agathê Tychê, Weimar.

himself to the Unique? Could he be alluding to his engagement to Lili Schönemann, who, as he told Eckermann when he learned of her death, had been ultimately the first and only woman he had loved "with a true, deep love"?[78] In his view, all his other inclinations were merely "light and superficial." One might also think of the spiritual marriage that linked him for several years to Charlotte von Stein. Yet I rather think that Goethe had in mind his liaison with Christiane Vulpius, which finally led to marriage, which would also explain the remarks in the commentary on the abdication of freedom that marriage demands, and that transforms inclination into "a thousand duties." On July 12, 1788, shortly after his return from the journey to Italy, Goethe met Christiane and immediately fell in love. They decided to live together, so that in 1796, Goethe could declare that "I am married, but without ceremony."[79] The two lovers developed the custom of celebrating this anniversary every year. Soon, however, this love collided with conventions and social prejudices. Christiane became pregnant, and brought a son into the world. Extramarital relations were against the law. For a while, the two lovers had to leave Goethe's house in Frauenplan and live outside the gates of the

FIGURE 5. Detail from page 10 of Otto van Veen, *Emblemata sive symbola a principibus, viris ecclesiasticis ac militaribus aliisque vsurpanda. Deuises ou emblemes pour princes, gens d'Eglise, gens de guerre, & aultres* (1624).

city. Christiane was to have four other children, in extremely painful childbirths, and all four died, almost immediately after their birth. She was the talk of Weimar high society. People made fun of Goethe's "maid." In 1806, after the battle of Jena, Napoleon's soldiers occupied Weimar and began looting: they attacked Goethe's house, and it was thanks to Christiane's courage and energy that they withdrew. A few days later, after almost twenty years of life in common, Goethe added the "ceremony" and married Christiane, who thus became, much to the annoyance of her detractors, "Madame secret counsellor." She was to die ten years later, in 1818, a year before the *Urworte* were written. Was Goethe thinking about his dead wife when he wrote: "That which is most cherished is scolded from our heart"?

Thus, Goethe had known the intoxication of the senses with Christiane, but also the joys and sufferings of family life, to which the stanza on Eros alludes. Some historians have considered that his liaison with Christiane had, in the long run, been stifling for Goethe, since she had neither the social rank nor the education required to be the great man's wife, and she gradually lost her charms; that she had "become ugly and vulgar." For instance, Friedrich Gundolf wrote in 1920: "Goethe paid dearly for having based a liaison that was to be lasting on an ephemeral state of affairs. He was no longer able to extricate himself from this liaison after it had lost its meaning." For Gundolf, Christiane corresponded perfectly to what Goethe needed after his return trip to Italy, but then she had become a useless burden. Gundolf goes on to cite the "poignant confession" in which, he claims, the poem "Amyntas" consists.[80] The reader will certainly excuse us for quoting this poem in its totality, because, in addition to its beauty, it shows that two themes from the Orphic poem were already on Goethe's mind in 1797: that of the will of nature as an inexorable power that imposes itself on human beings, and that of the demands and sacrifices that any love imposes.

Nicias, excellent man, physician of body and soul!
I am truly ill, but your remedy is harsh.

Ah! my strength to follow your advice has dwindled.
Yes, and my friend now seems like an opponent to me.
I cannot gainsay you; I tell myself everything,
Tell myself even the word, more harsh, that you do keep silent.
Yet, alas! The water pours down the precipitous cliff,
In haste, and songs halt not the waves of the brook.
Does the storm not rage inexorably? And does the Sun
Not roll down from the peak of the day to the waves?
Thus, from all around me, nature says: "You too, Amyntas,
Are bent 'neath the strict law of the powers of bronze."
Wrinkle your brow no more, my friend, and hear with good will
What a tree taught me yesterday, there, by the brook.
Once so heavily laden, it now brings me few apples:
See, the ivy that embraces it so powerfully is to blame.
And I seized the sharp, crooked knife,
Severed and cut, tore down vine after vine,
Yet I soon shuddered when, with a deep, pathetic sigh,
A whispered lament poured forth from the treetops:
"Oh, do not harm me, your faithful garden companion,
To whom, as a boy, you owed so many early pleasures.
Oh, do not harm me! With this web, which you violently destroy,
You cruelly tear my life tear away from me!
Have I not nourished it myself and gently brought it up for myself?
Are its leaves not akin to me, as are my own?
Shall I not love the plant, which, needing me alone,
Silently, with avid strength, coils itself around my flanks?
A thousand vines have taken root; with thousands upon thousands
Of fibers, it sinks firmly into my life.
It takes nourishment from me; what I needed, it enjoys;
And thus it sucks the marrow, sucks out the soul from me.
Only in vain do I still feed myself: my powerful roots
Send up only half the living sap—Alas!
For the dangerous guest, most beloved, nimbly lays claim,
Along the way, to the strength of autumn fruits.

Nothing reaches my crown; the highest treetops
Wither; already, the branch over the brook withers away.
Yes, she is a traitress, she coaxes life and possessions from me;
Coaxes from me my striving force, my hope.
She is all I feel, she alone, the entwining one; in these bonds alone
      do I delight,
In this fatal adornment, this foreign foliage."
Hold back your knife, O Nicias! Spare the poor one,
Who, willingly forced, consumes himself in loving pleasure!
All profligacy is sweet; Oh! Let me enjoy the most beautiful one!
He who entrusts himself to love: does he pay heed to his life?[81]

The poem was written during a period, autumn 1797, in which
some disagreements had arisen between Christiane and Goethe,
brought about in particular by the poet's frequent absences. This is
why it is generally accepted that it contains allusions to their life as
a couple.[82] However, this is no "poignant confession" but a carefully
studied, well-mulled-over poem, written with a clear head, so to
speak. The first verses, for instance, are inspired by the Cyclops of
the Greek poet Theocritus, who also addresses a personage called
Nicias, a doctor but also a poet, telling him that there is no other
remedy for love than poetry.[83] If we assume that the poem refers to
Christiane, Nicias might represent Schiller, in whom Goethe sensed
a deep hostility with regard to his liaison with Christiane. Amyntas,
whom Goethe uses as his interpreter, admits what he calls his illness,
which is none other than love. He immediately rejects the remedy
proposed by Nicias, i.e., separation, by appealing to the inflexible
law and necessity of nature, whose irresistible course cannot be
stopped: the flow of a waterfall or a brook, the force of a storm, or
the reflection of the sun on the water. Amyntas, too, is subject to the
inflexible power of fate. He is like the apple tree, which is invaded by
ivy but, because of their common growth and intimate union, cannot live without it. Goethe had noted in his diary on September 19,
1797, that he had noticed a tree choked by ivy. Far from a poignant

lamentation, however, the poem ultimately expresses consent to fate and, above all, a great tenderness for the beloved object. This is what Wilhelm von Humboldt had noticed, when he wrote to Goethe:

> The passage: Shall I not love the plant, etc., produces a wonderful effect. Never could one describe, in a stronger, more true way, the intimacy by means of which one being is incorporated into another being, and makes this foreign nourishment and life its own.[84]

Yet it is especially the end of the poem that must attract our attention. Here, Amyntas depicts himself as a voluntary slave, who consumes himself in the pleasure of loving. This reminds us of the maxim we cited above, "Voluntary dependence is the most beautiful situation; and how could it be possible without love?": every attachment to a human being engenders obligations and dependency with regard to her.[85] Originally, the poem ended with the following two verses:

> All profligacy is sweet; the most beautiful of all is, when the girl grants it to us, to sacrifice everything for her.

In the definitive version, written two years later, the idea of sacrifice disappears:

> All profligacy is sweet; Oh! Let me enjoy the most beautiful one! He who entrusts himself to love: does he pay heed to his life?

For Goethe, then, extravagance is sweet, because it presupposes that one gives away the wealth one possesses, and ultimately that one give oneself away. Thus, in the masquerade of the first act of *Faust II*, the young charioteer proclaims:

> I am Extravagance, I am Poetry, I am the Poet who perfects himself when he squanders his most intimate possession.[86]

The most beautiful extravagance is thus the gift of oneself through love, which does not even try to spare its life: "To renounce oneself is enjoyment," as Goethe was to say in the poem "One and All," one of those that best reveal Goethe's philosophy.[87]

Ultimately, the poem "Amyntas," if it was written about Christiane, expresses love and tenderness, not lassitude. The most recent studies on Christiane have, moreover, corrected Gundolf's exaggerations and better defined the exact nature of the relation between the poet and the woman he had always loved.[88] Their correspondence testifies to a close mutual understanding in the most diverse fields. Goethe often associated Christiane with his literary production and dedicated to her his beautiful poem "The Metamorphosis of Plants," in which human love is frequently mentioned.

Ultimately, the *Urworte*, in their conclusion, have nothing very precise to tell us about Goethe's life, and his amorous life in particular, and nothing allows us to affirm, as Charles Du Bos nevertheless does, that Christiane was, quite specifically, a kind of trap that had been set for him by Anankê.[89] In fact, the poem is situated in a universal viewpoint and defines the phases of human life and the powers that are linked to them: the Daimôn to birth, Tukhê to childhood and youth, Eros to adolescence and maturity, and Anankê to old age. The four lots enumerated by Macrobius enabled Goethe to sketch the constellation of forces that had determined the entire course of his existence.

The Caduceus

After this lengthy detour, let us return to the text of Macrobius, which seems to have provided Goethe with only a general framework to express his ideas on human destiny. So far, however, we have said little about an essential element of Macrobius's text, the figure of the caduceus. Without appearing explicitly, might this figure not be secretly present in the structure of the poem?

Let us recall Macrobius's description of the caduceus. It appears in the form of two entwined serpents, male and female. They are Daimôn and Tukhê, Sun and Moon. Their mouths are joined in a kiss that represents Eros. The front parts of their bodies form a circle, while the middle portions of their bodies are tightly tied in a knot that Macrobius calls the knot of Heracles, renowned in antiquity for being very hard to untie.[90] This knot is Anankê. From here, the lower parts of their bodies form a final circle, with their extremities uniting on the handle, at a point where two wings have their origin (figure 6). For Macrobius, each detail of the figure of the caduceus thus corresponds to one of the divinities that determine human destiny. However, he does not give a name to the wings, contenting himself with saying: "Why the wings are added, we have already said." Indeed, a few pages earlier, he has recognized the power of the mind in the wings that are attributed to Mercury. Goethe had read in Zoega's dissertation that "All is subject to him [to Anankê], except the indomitable audacity of the human spirit, which we call, by another name, Hope." For Goethe, Hope is a winged being, who gives us wings.

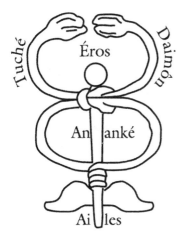

FIGURE 6. Caduceus of Macrobius.

I believe this figure can help us to understand the structure of the poem. One might say that there is, first of all, a horizontal dimension: the opposition and entwining of the two serpents, so that the stanza devoted to the Daimôn is opposed to the one dedicated to Tukhê. Then there is a vertical dimension: Eros corresponds to the kiss of the two serpents, and, as Goethe says, he is the result of the encounter between Daimôn and Tukhê. This is why he is located on the central axis of the figure. Likewise, Anankê corresponds to the knot of Hercules, that is, to the close interlacing between Daimôn and Tukhê. Finally, Elpis, who, for Goethe, corresponds to the wings, is situated on the same axis, since these two wings originate on the handle. There is thus an opposition, on the one hand between Eros and Anankê, between free choice and constraint, and, on the other, between Anankê and Elpis, between imprisonment within limits and flight toward the infinite.

It may be of interest to note that Alastair Fowler discerns a similar influence of Macrobius's text on the first four books of Spenser's *The Faerie Queene*.[91] According to Fowler, books 1 and 2 of Spenser's poem correspond to Macrobius's Daimôn and Tukhê, and hence to the Sun and the Moon. Book 3 is devoted to Eros, and book 4 to Necessity, and hence to Mercury. Thus, in book 4, the figure of the caduceus, which appears in 4.3, 42, connects all the powers of generation, and the reconciliation between Britomart and Arthegall (6.6) is the precise equivalent of the meeting of the solar and lunar principles in the caduceus. Here, however, Hope is lacking.

In Goethe's poem, at any rate, this Hope appears as a power that surpasses and transcends all others. If the wings of the caduceus represent it, these wings should be located at the top, and not, as in Macrobius, at the bottom of the caduceus. In fact, this figure, known from immemorial times in the Indo-European tradition, can assume many forms.[92] Since Greco-Roman antiquity, some caducei bore wings that were located at the summit of the shaft (figure 7).

In a previous study, I had thought a parallel could be established

FIGURE 7. Caduceus, Musée de
Saint-Germain-en-Laye.

between the theme of the caduceus and another theme dear to
Goethe: that of spirality in the world of plants.[93] Since then, however, it has occurred to me that in the theme of the spirality of plants,
the spiral represents the feminine element, which is opposed to masculine verticality. In the caduceus, by contrast, there is indeed an
opposition between the spirality of the serpents and the verticality
of the shaft or the handle. Yet of the two serpents themselves, one
is feminine and the other masculine, since they correspond to the
Sun and the Moon, to the Daimôn and to Tukhê. The models do not
coincide. At most, one could recognize in the figure of the caduceus
the two great motive forces which, according to Goethe, are at work
in natural processes: polarity (*Polarität*) and ascent (*Steigerung*).[94]
The two serpents, Daimôn and Tukhê, correspond to the opposition between contraries that are reconciled in love. Hope, which
transcends Necessity, would then correspond to the movement of
perpetual ascent which, for Goethe, is proper to the Spirit.[95]

Elpis, Hope

The stanza devoted to Elpis is quite different from the preceding four stanzas. They allude to life events: birth, adolescent frequentations, marriage, the difficult life of an elderly man. In contrast, Elpis appears as a being who rises upward, above the clouds and the rain, traversing space and transcending temporality.[96]

We have said that Goethe probably thought of Hope when he read in Zoega's dissertation: "All is subject to her [to Anankê] save the indomitable audacity of the human spirit which we call, by another name, Hope."[97] Here, L. G. Zoega, the scholar, archaeologist, and numismatist, expressed himself in a rather surprising way. It is true that antiquity recognized the indomitable audacity of the human spirit, discovering it, first of all, in the temerity displayed by technical inventions. Before enumerating these, the chorus of Sophocles's *Antigone* exclaims:

Many things are formidable, and none more formidable than man![98]

Above all, the ancients saw this audacity in the adventure of a mind that seeks to transcend the limits of the world. As Seneca was to say:

How closely in accord with nature it is to let one's mind reach out into the boundless universe![99]

The anonymous treatise *On the Sublime* echoes Seneca:

Nature . . . has breathed into our hearts an unconquerable passion for whatever is great and more divine than ourselves. Thus the whole universe is not enough to satisfy the contemplation and discursive thought of human apprehension; our thoughts often pass beyond the limits that confine us.[100]

In contrast, I do not know any text—unless I am mistaken—that affirms that the audacity of the spirit triumphs over Necessity. At most, one may admit that this impulse toward the infinite allows human beings to free themselves from the limits imposed upon them.

Above all, what is rather enigmatic in Zoega's text is that he affirms that "we"—that is, the moderns—call the audacity of the spirit "Hope." First of all, this does not correspond to the Christian notion of Hope, which concerns survival and resurrection and was widely diffused in the time of Zoega and Goethe, for it bears no relation to the audacity of the spirit. Insofar as he speaks of the audacity of the spirit, therefore, Zoega seems to have been influenced by the spirit of the "Enlightenment," whose motto, according to Kant, was *Sapere aude* (dare to know, dare to think for yourself), and which thus considered the "indomitable audacity of the spirit" as the supreme value.[101] However, the Enlightenment does not seem to have established a link between audacity and the spirit of hope. At most, one could find a mention of "hopes" in the plural in Condorcet, with regard to the adventure of the human spirit.[102]

In any case, it may be useful to specify what the word *Elpis* meant for the Greeks. In archaic Greece, in the eighth century BCE, the word appears, in particular, in the famous passage of the poet Hesiod that tells how Zeus, who wished to avenge the theft of fire by Prometheus, sent among humans the seductive woman Pandora, whom each of the gods had contributed to fashioning (hence the name Pandora, which, according to Hesiod, means "gift of all the gods," i.e., to humanity). She brought a jar with her, and when she removed the lid, all kinds of evils escaped from it and came to attack human beings. When she closed the lid once again—by the will of Zeus, as Hesiod says—all that was left in the jar was Hope.[103] In fact, the meaning of this myth is not quite clear. In the first place, one may think, with Simina Noica, that Elpis does not necessarily mean "Hope,"[104] for when one studies the usages of the verb *elpizô* in Homer, one may conclude that the Greek root *elp-* can designate a threefold relation, or a triple "opening": toward something negative, toward a neutral situation, and toward a favorable situation. Hence, it is a faculty of opening up to all situations: "This is what finally remains in Pandora's *pithos*, once all the evils have flown away: this original maneuver, expressing a human being's basic opening-up," which makes her capable of confronting every situation.[105]

What, moreover, does it mean that, by the will of Zeus, as Hesiod emphasizes, Elpis remains in the jar? In that case, one can wonder whether it is possible for human beings to have access to it. If that is impossible, then Zeus wanted to deprive human beings of hope; if it is possible, then from the perspective of Zeus's vengeance, it is a deceptive hope that hides the reality of their fate from them.[106] Much later, in the second or third century of our era, the fabulist Babrius proposes a very different version of the myth: the jar contains only good things that are sent by Zeus, but they immediately fly away to Olympus and escape the grasp of human beings.[107] All that remains for them is hope, for people believe that it will provide them with the good things that escape from them. One can already glimpse this version in Theognis, in the sixth century BCE. For him, the beneficent divinities—Good Faith, Wisdom, the Graces—have fled from the earth and gone back to Olympus. The only beneficent divinity left among human beings is Hope.[108]

Yet Hope retained an ambiguous value down to the end of antiquity, as consolation or as deceptive illusion, as we can see from this poem of the *Palatine Anthology*, which may allude to the lots of human destiny:

> Farewell, Hope and Fortune, a long farewell. I have found my harbor. I have no more to do with you. Fool those who come after me.[109]

Goethe took up the myth of Pandora, albeit profoundly transformed, not only in an eponymous text published in 1810, but also in the project for a second part, of which we possess a plan written in Goethe's hand on May 18, 1808: it was to be called "The Return of Pandora."[110] In the published version, Epimetheus and Prometheus are discussing their memory of the beauty of Pandora, who has abandoned Epimetheus. The latter, remembering the episode of the jar, describes a situation that would correspond to the Hellenistic version of the myth. Seductive images—of happiness in love, or of elegance, for instance—escape from the vase like a cloud of incense. Human beings try to grasp them, but they slip away, so that, although Epimetheus does not say so explicitly, all that is left for them is Hope, which is nothing but the vain, illusory pursuit of risky or inaccessible good things.[111] This, moreover, is the meaning of the two names Goethe gives to Pandora's two daughters: Epimeleia (Care) and Elpore (Hope). In the play, Elpore appears as a women who, although gracious and kind, is nevertheless ungraspable and flighty, and who declares: "Promising what is impossible suits me."[112] When she disappears from Epimetheus's sight, he cries out: "How sweetly do you dissolve, O beautiful world of dreams!"[113]

For Goethe, as Cassirer has rightly shown, Pandora represents Beauty as an ideal, creative Form in the Platonic and especially Plotinian sense. Since it has abandoned the earth, the ideal is merely a dream, and life has been invaded by violence, as is shown by the episode of Phileros, who wants to kill Epimeleia, whom he loves and of whom he is jealous. Ultimately, Hope is nothing but a mere illusion.

Judging by the very brief sketch Goethe made of the second part,[114] it was intended to describe the transformation of humanity by the return of Pandora. This time, Pandora is not content to meet the two Titans, Epimetheus and Prometheus, but she is now surrounded "by winemakers, fishermen, farmers, and shepherds"—by working people, one might say—each of whom receives the influences and gifts of Pandora in their own way. This means that the ideal Form, which, for Goethe, is the law of nature and the moral law, will be embodied in the immense variety of human acts. Here we can glimpse, expressed in the disguise of ancient myth, the modern, perhaps Masonic hope of a transformation of humanity by the gifts of Pandora, which, according to an indication of the all-too-brief sketch that Goethe has left us, could be "art and science." Happiness must be sought in action, in creation, inspired by the ideal, or by an effective, concrete involvement in social life. Here, as Ernst Cassirer remarks, we find the deep modification that took place in Goethe's old age, for instance in *Wilhelm Meister's Journeyman Years*, or at the end of the *Second Faust*.[115] The goal of life is no longer the realization of personal perfection but action in the service of the human community.

With this return of Pandora, Hope is completely transformed. Goethe's sketch envisaged that at the end of the play, Elpore addresses the spectators, but under the name of Elpore *thraseia*, "bold Hope," self-confident, the Hope of men of action, creative and inspired.

Goethe was careful not to comment on the stanza he had dedicated to Hope, leaving it up to the reader herself to provide a "moral and religious commentary." Perhaps he wished to respect the idea that his readers themselves had of Hope: he contents himself with saying, "You know her well." It is true that a few years earlier, he had taken care to give voice to Hope herself, to make her proclaim her powers and her qualities: in fact, she appears in the musical situation piece entitled *The Awakening of Epimenides*, which Goethe composed on the occasion of the Allied victory over Napoleon in 1815. Stronger than her two sisters, Faith and Charity, whom the Demon of Oppression has managed to chain up, she alone resists him and delivers the two prisoners. In this context, she defines herself as follows:

> Yes, whoever conspires with me
> Is aware of all happiness!
> For as I am now, so am I constantly,
> Never do I yield to despair;
> I lessen pain; the highest happiness, I make complete;
> Female in form, I am brave as a man;

Life itself lives through me alone,
Yes, I can extend it beyond the grave.[116]

We recognize bold Hope, the Elpore *thraseia* of the "Return of
Pandora," and as E. Trunz remarks, we find here a summary of the
way Goethe represents Hope to himself, and especially the idea that
Hope is inherent in life.[117] The reason is probably that for him, life
is a force of ascent (*Steigerung*), an impulse that ceaselessly seeks
to transcend itself. Nevertheless, the Hope of the *Urworte* does not
resemble either the Elpore *thraseia* of the "Return of Pandora," or
the Hope who speaks in the *Awakening of Epimenides*. The Hope of
the *Urworte* is a being who, free of all constraint, soars like a bird
"above the ceiling of the clouds, the fog, the rainstorms." "It grants
us wings and raises us up with it / You know it well! It swarms
through all the spaces! / One beat of its wings, and the eons are
behind us." Hope is a being who escapes the limits and bronze barriers of Necessity. If, this time, Goethe evokes the wings of Hope, it
is because he is thinking of the wings of Hermes's caduceus, which,
for Macrobius, represented the agility of the spirit.

Yet haven't we already encountered this being that floats and
flies? Wasn't it the Genius, floating between heaven and earth, who
personified "the contemplation of and meditation on what is above
and what is below"? Wasn't it poetry as well, which, for Goethe,
is an ascending force, comparable to a bird or a balloon, inciting
Euphorion, the son of Helen and Faust, to leap higher and higher?
Poetry, which "like a profane Gospel, delivers us from earthly heaviness"?[118] Might this profane Gospel, this good news, not be Hope?[119]

The Floating Genius, ultimately a symbol of poetry, said, while
looking down toward the earth from above:

Every day and every night
Thus I praise the lot of humankind:
If he always thinks of what is Right,
He is always beautiful and great.

If this flight of the mind leads to "praising the lot of human-kind," whereas the succession of powers that rule human destiny—Daimôn, Tukhê, Eros, Anankê—finally gave rise to a feeling of oppression and captivity, it is because the flight of the mind provides a new vision of that destiny. Such is the virtue of gazing upward and downward: this higher vision delivers us from the partial and particular viewpoint of the individual. A text from Nietzsche, which we have already cited, helps us to understand how this elevation allows us to transcend Necessity:

> All that is necessary, seen from above and in the sense of a *great* economy, is also what is useful in itself. We must not merely put up with it: we must *love* it.[120]

Obviously, the stanza on Hope does not express in detail how the flight of Hope delivers us from Necessity. Yet everything Goethe has said about poetry, "which brings us serenity," helps us to give voice to it. In this context, moreover, poetry represents not a literary genre practiced by a writer, but an attitude, or a spiritual exercise characterized by that movement of detachment from oneself that transforms our thought and our action, a transformation of the relation to the real, a "transfiguration of the everyday," in the words of Goethe's commentary on the *Book of Paradise* in the *West-Eastern Divan*:

> A transfigured everyday lends us wings to reach the higher and the highest. And what could prevent the poet from mounting the wonderful horse of Muhammed and soaring throughout heaven?[121]

This wonderful horse reminds us of Pegasus, the winged horse, symbol of poetry, which, as Theo Buch reminds us, was depicted on the reverse of a medal by Schadow in honor of Goethe in 1816.[122]

This view from above, which resituates destiny within the perspective of the All, the Cosmos, and universal existence, then leads

to an assent to existence, considered as the supreme value, to a complete consent to the will of God-Nature, to a "joyous fatalism," as
Nietzsche was to say with regard to Goethe.[123] From the heights of
his tower, Lynceus sang at the end of the *Second Faust*:

> Be it as it will,
> It was so lovely!

As early as 1780, in the poem "My Goddess," Hope appeared as
she who "nobly stimulates and consoles," and hence incites to action.
Goethe, who called her his silent friend, made her the daughter of
Zeus and the sister of Phantasy, or Imagination, and ultimately of
Poetry, whom Zeus gave to human beings so that they might be
delivered from the yoke of necessity.[124]

Obviously, this being who flies beyond time and space could be
a Hope that carries us into the spaces of another life. Goethe firmly
believed in the possibility for human action to be prolonged and
intensified in higher spheres of existence:

> For me, the conviction of our survival emanates from the concept
> of activity. If, until my end, I am active without a moment's rest,
> nature is obliged to assign another form of existence to me, if the
> present form can no longer suffice for my spirit.[125]

In fact, one could point out, with Walter Benjamin, that this idea
of survival is not a hope in Goethe, since he considers that nature
owes it to him to grant him another form of existence.[126] Yet doesn't
Benjamin here conceive of hope too exclusively after the Christian
model, according to which hope presupposes divine grace? In fact,
Goethe never had much enthusiasm for the hope of the "pious,"
especially if one can judge by a passage from the *Conversations with
Eckermann*. Here, Goethe admits that it would be fine by him to have
the chance to live another life, after the end of life on this earth, but
that he would only request not to meet up with any of the pious who

believed in the immortality of the soul while they were down here below, and who would say: "Well, didn't it happen?" Otherwise, he would be condemned to endless boredom. Concerning oneself with the immortality of the soul is good for people who have nothing to do. But a person who works and acts "leaves the future world alone, and is content to be active and useful in this one."[127]

In any case, one might think that the Hope of the *Urworte* delivers human beings from Necessity by opening up the spaces of the Beyond for them. Yet I find it hard to accept that, for Goethe in the *Urworte*, human destiny is reduced to the earthly defeat that results from the triumph of Anankê, and is immediately followed by an escape into the beyond. Goethe was too faithful to the earth to imagine things in this way. That is why I understand Hope in the *Urworte* as a power that, by drawing us upward, enables us to reinterpret the destiny that is imposed on us, and to act confidently, situating our action within the perspective of the All and of the will of God-Nature. Hope is inherent in life and in action. To hope is to be alive, to be active. It is significant that the last instant of Faust's existence is illuminated by Hope. He hopes to dry up swamps, thereby granting land to millions of human beings:

> I would like to stand on free land, with a free people;
> Then could I say to the Instant:
> Stay! You are so beautiful!
> The trace of my earthly years
> cannot be destroyed in the ages.
> In anticipation of such happiness
> I now enjoy the highest instant![128]

Here, Hope is the project of activity, an activity devoted to the transformation and the happiness of humanity, like the one we glimpsed when recalling "The Return of Pandora." This vision of the future can reach the intensity of a pregnant instant, in which Instant and Eternity meet.

Ultimately, Hope in the *Urworte* corresponds to that audacity of the spirit of which Zoega spoke, which, resituating the individual within the perspective of the All, enables her to always act confidently, ever more intensely, in the perpetual effort to ascend that is inherent in life.

4

The Yes to Life and the World

Throughout these pages, whether the subject has been concentration on the present, the view from above, or hope, we have repeatedly come across a fundamental leitmotif: the joyous consent to life and to existence in the world, or the joy of existing. With regard to concentration on the present, we evoked the verses from the *Divan*: "Great is the joy of being there. Greater still is the joy one feels in existence itself,"[1] or this passage from the *Testament*: "Let reason be present wherever life rejoices in life."[2] As far as the view from above is concerned, Lynceus, from the top of his tower, sang a hymn to the universal adornment:

My fortunate eyes:
Whate'er you have seen,
Be it as it will,
It was so lovely!

And the stanza from the *Floating Genius*, which opposes the *Memento mori* ("Think of death") of the Platonists and Christians to the *Memento vivere* ("Think of living,"[3] "Don't forget to live") of Spinoza, reminded us of the inscription mentioned in *Wilhelm*

Meister's Journeyman Years: "Don't forget to live."⁴ Finally, Hope implies, as we have seen, a consent to existence and to being-in-the-world.

Great Is the Joy of Being-There (*Freude des Daseins*)⁵

This joy in existing is, first of all, an immediate, almost unconscious feeling. Goethe describes it in his praise of Winckelmann, written in 1805, which gave him the opportunity to praise the way in which, unlike the Romantics and Christianity, the ancient Greeks knew how to exist.

> If the healthy nature of mankind . . . feels itself to be in the world as if in a Whole that is great, beautiful, worthy, and valuable; if harmonious pleasure provides him with a pure, free delight; then the universe, if it could be conscious of itself, would shout with joy, having reached its goal, and it would marvel at this summit of its becoming and its being.

Goethe explains his thought in these famous lines:

> For what good is all this extravagance of suns, planets, and moons, of stars and milky ways, comets, nebulas, worlds that have become and are becoming, if finally one happy person does not rejoice unconsciously at her own existence?⁶

Obviously, we find here the anthropomorphic vision of a universe whose goal is mankind, that being who is microscopic compared with the immensity of the cosmos. It is true, however, that for us human beings, what gives meaning to the universe is that spontaneous joy which, for us, is linked to existence, and to the fact of "feeling oneself in the world as in a whole." And in order for us to exist, all this exuberance of suns and nebulas is necessary.

We feel this joy of existing, as it were, without any reason, for we understand nothing of the enigma of the world. Goethe compares

it to a child's pleasure when savoring what he likes. As he remarked
in a conversation with Eckermann of February 28, 1831:

> We suffer and rejoice in accordance with eternal laws, we accom-
> plish them and they accomplish themselves in us, whether we
> know them or not. Doesn't a child like a cake, although he knows
> nothing about the pastry-cook, and doesn't a starling like cherries,
> without reflecting on how they were produced?[7]

The great laws of nature (those of the *Urworte*, one might add),
those laws of bronze that dominate us, transcend our understanding. Yet the unreflecting, pure joy of a child or an animal is a sign
or a symbol of this unfathomable mystery. One thinks of this brief
poem by Hölderlin:

> Little knowledge, but much joy,
> has been granted to mortals.
> Why, o beautiful sun, are you not enough
>   for me,
> flower of my flowers, on a day in May?
> What do I know that is higher?
> Oh, that I were like children!
> That I, like the nightingale, might sing
> a carefree song of my joy![8]

If Goethe speaks of children and starlings, it is because there
was a proverb he liked to quote: "One must ask children and starlings about the taste of cherries and currants." He seems to have
understood it in different ways. In *Poetry and Truth*, when discussing the *System of Nature* by Baron d'Holbach, a depressing book by
a depressed old man, the proverb means that it is beings full of life
whom one must ask for the taste for life and the spontaneous joy
of existence.[9] In a passage from the *Conversations with Eckermann*,

by contrast, the proverb seems to mean simply that there's no use arguing about tastes and colors.[10]

For Goethe, reality and existence are thus inseparable from the joy of existing.[11] Being-there (*Dasein*) rejoices in its being-there, or its existence. In a letter to Schiller, he writes:

> Pleasure, joy, participation in things: that is the only reality, and all that produces reality. All else is vanity, and merely traps us.[12]

This joy inherent in existing is an *Urphänomen*, an originary phenomenon that allows a glimpse of what cannot be explored. Eckermann situates the conversation we have reported within the perspective of a discussion of God, or the supreme Being:

> Goethe himself is far from believing that he knows the supreme Being as He is. All his affirmations, written and oral, indicate that He is something unfathomable, of which humankind has only approximate traces and sense. Nature, moreover, and all of us, are so permeated by the divine that it contains us, and we live, move, and have our being in it.[13]

These last words are an allusion to the famous speech of Saint Paul on the Areopagus:[14]

> He is not far from each of us, for it is in Him that we live, that we move, and that we have our being, and, as some of your poets have said, "We are of His race."[15]

Goethe obviously appreciated the reference to the Greek poets, but he interprets this phrase rather in the sense of pantheism. For him, the fact that we are thus permeated with the divine means that we act, suffer, and derive enjoyment according to laws that are incomprehensible to us.

Greater Still Is the Joy One Feels in Existence Itself (*Freude am Dasein*)[16]

Above this spontaneous and unconscious joy that an existent feels in a given moment of existence, there is, says Goethe, a greater joy: that which the existent, now aware of its existence, experiences in the very fact of existing, and feels for life itself, whatever the circumstances of this life may be. What fills us with joy is the "feeling of existence" so well described by Rousseau, and which we have already mentioned.[17] The object of this feeling is not any specific pleasant moment, but pure existence, taken in itself. We have just said: "whatever the circumstances may be." Thus, Lynceus ended his hymn to universal adornment with these words:

My fortunate eyes:
Whate'er you have seen,
Be it as it will,
It was so lovely!

As we have said, it seems that the restriction "Be it as it will" is an allusion to the tragic spectacle that Lynceus is about to discover, the burning of the hut of Philemon and Baucis, caused against Faust's will by Mephistopheles's brutality in carrying out his orders.[18] We find an analogous restriction in the last verse of the poem "The Fiancé": "Whatever it may be, life is beautiful."[19] Among other things, this poem evokes his broken engagement with Lili Schönemann and her death. This was the Lili who, as Goethe told Eckermann, had been the greatest love of his life, a love he considered "demonic" because it had oriented his destiny.[20] This last verse is, as it were, the calm gaze of an old man on his life and on life, although traversed by breakups, heartbreaks, and mourning. On his life and on life, for the fiancé does not say "life was good," but "life is good, not only my life, but life, or existence in itself."

Yet how is it possible for Lynceus to say that, whatever his eyes may have seen—and they have seen the tragic end of Philemon and Baucis—it was so beautiful, and for the fiancé to find that life is good, despite its dramas and sufferings? The answer is that in Goethe's view, reality is good and beautiful, even if it is a mixture of happiness and suffering. In fact, Goethe never had any illusions about human beings or nature. Mephistopheles points out to God that mankind use their reason to make themselves worse than animals.[21] And Goethe has Werther say: "A devouring monster is hidden in all of nature."[22] In a youthful work, Goethe makes the following remark:

> Are furious storms, floods, rains of fire, subterranean lava, and death in all the elements not just as true witnesses to the eternal life of nature as the sun rising magnificently over opulent vineyards and fragrant groves of orange trees? . . . What we see of nature is force devouring force; nothing present, everything passing, a thousand seeds ruined, a thousand seeds born every instant . . . beautiful and ugly, good and evil, everything existing side by side, with equal justification.[23]

The Yes to Becoming and the Terrifying

In Goethe, we can observe the will to consent to the most problematic aspects of existence: on the one hand, to the becoming of being, its perpetual metamorphosis; and, on the other, to all that is distressing and terrifying in reality.

First, being is perpetual creation and destruction. In order to be, one must accept change and death:

> The eternal stirs in all things / For all must dissolve into nothingness, if it would persevere in being.[24]

When Goethe says, "keep yourself attached to being with delight," he means: let yourself be swept into creative and destructive

movement of eternal essence.[25] This movement is described in these
two stanzas of "One and All":

> And to transform all that is created
> Lest it be fixed in hostile rigidity
> Eternal, living action is at work
> And what was not, now wills to become
> Pure Suns, colorful Earths;
> In no case may it rest.
> It must stir, act creatively,
> First take form, then transform,
> Only in appearance does it stand still for a moment.
> The eternal keeps stirring in all things,
> for all must dissolve into nothingness,
> Would it persevere in being.

One could speak here of a kind of mystical experience that is
expressed several times in various poems, first and foremost in
the opening stanza of the poem "One and All," which we have just
quoted:

> To find himself in the Infinite,
> The individual shall willingly disappear,
> There, all weariness dissolves.
> Instead of ardent desire, and savage will,
> Troublesome demand, and rigorous constraint,
> It is a pleasure to surrender.[26]

As Roger Ayrault has noted in the valuable commentary he gives
on this poem, we find an echo of the *Urworte* here in this mention
of "ardent desire," which could be Eros, and of "rigorous constraint,"
which could be Necessity.[27] These are the limits from which the individual liberates herself to reach the infinite. Roger Ayrault rightly
concludes that this transcendence of limits corresponds to "a pure

power of the spirit, a conscious disposition on the part of the individual to free herself, in spite of everything, from her original limitation, to 'disappear' in the sense of 'renouncing oneself,' sacrificing one's own personality, to no longer think of oneself as anything other than as a part of universal life."[28]

Unlike Roger Ayrault, however, I think that the description of transcending limits in the first stanza of "One and All" corresponds quite closely to the role played by Hope in the *Urworte*. For it is not so much a flight beyond death, as a power that enables one, by transcending individuality, to find a new mode of vision, a new mode of action, and to rediscover oneself by losing oneself in the All.

I would also be inclined to see in it a description of the experience that has been called the "oceanic feeling" since Freud and Romain Rolland.[29] It had already been described by Rousseau, among others:

> I feel ineffable ecstasies, raptures as I merge, as it were, into the system of beings, and identify myself with the whole of nature.[30]

The individual has the impression of dissolving, of transcending her limits in the immensity and infinity of reality, becoming aware of her communion with that All of which she is a part, and in this impression of dissolution she feels an immense joy: "It is a pleasure to surrender." She loses herself, and at the same time rediscovers herself in a higher state, in her feeling of belonging to the infinity of being.

We find the same theme in the poem "Blessed Nostalgia," which evokes a butterfly attracted by the light which consumes itself in the flame:

> Until you have understood
> This: die and become!
> You are naught but a gloomy guest
> on the dark earth.[31]

To understand this "die and become" is to consent to being's law of becoming, which demands that beings renounce their individuality in order to be able to achieve a higher level of existence, to commune with God/Nature. One could speak, in this regard, of death by love, for the poem, alluding to the butterfly's attraction to the light, addresses it as follows: "A new desire pushes you toward a higher wedding."

Another aspect of this "die and become," and this death by love, seems to be present at the end of the second act of *Faust II*. Homunculus, the figure of a man created by the artifices of alchemy, who can survive only in the narrow confines of a vial, tries to free himself in order to live with a body. Instigated by Eros and fascinated by the beauty of Galatea, he breaks his glass envelope by smashing into the foot of her throne, and spreads and dissolves in the aquatic elements, which will enable him to go through the stages of Nature's evolution and becoming. He thus finds himself in a new state within Nature.

Goethe, moreover, insists strongly and constantly on the anguish-inducing aspects of existence. He himself was deeply anxious, particularly in the face of death. For instance, he did not have the courage to be present at his wife's painful agony.[32] Yet he accepted anguish as a feeling that is, as it were, natural to human beings. Perhaps he was influenced on this point by Schelling, who spoke of the "sacred terror" mankind feels at the fact of existence, and for whom "anguish" was "the fundamental feeling of every creature."[33] What makes existence anguish-inducing is, first, the death implied by Being's eternal becoming, but it is also the enigmatic nature of existence, the limits we encounter in the knowledge of nature, and the impenetrable mystery it allows us to glimpse. Reality cannot be expressed in human language or discourse:

We talk too much. We should talk less, and draw more. For my part, I would like to give up speaking and continue to express myself like formative Nature, in still drawings. That fig tree, this little snake, the cocoon . . . all these are "signatures," full of content. Yes, he who could decipher their meaning correctly, would soon be able to do without everything written and spoken. The more I think about it, the more it seems to me that there is something so useless, idle, and even, I would say, fatuous in speech, that one is frightened by the quiet seriousness and silence of nature.[34]

In Nature, Goethe sees a gushing forth of visible forms, or "phenomena" in the sense of "apparitions," which language is incapable of expressing. Why is he terrified by them? Because these forms are, as it were, the "signatures" of something ineffable, unknown, and unexplorable. Forms are the "symbol," that is, the "revelation in life, and the instant of the unexplorable."[35] Knowledge of nature consists in arriving at what he calls "originary phenomena," which reveal to us the laws of the development of forms, but which are themselves forms that one cannot go beyond. This limitation, this inkling of the unexplorable, give rise to anguish:

The awareness of originary phenomena plunges us into a kind of anguish . . . before an originary phenomenon, when it appears unveiled to our senses, we feel a kind of awe that can go as far as anguish.[36]

Even more generally, there is something monstrous and terrifying (*ungeheuer*) in existence, because of what is completely inexplicable in it. Goethe considers that a human being is truly a human being only when she is capable of totally assuming that anguish in the face of the mystery of existence:

Yet it is not in paralysis that I seek my salvation.
The shudder of terror is the best part of man
However dearly the world may make him pay for this feeling,
Gripped, he feels what is dreadful [*das Ungeheuer*] in his inner
    depths.[37]

Goethe and Nietzsche

It has long been noticed that in Goethe, this concept of being as creation and destruction, but also this transcendence of individuality, this sense of mystery, this presentiment of Dionysian ecstasy, herald Nietzsche, whom they were to influence.[38] Speaking explicitly of Goethe, Nietzsche himself describes Goethe's assent to existence, in all that is wonderful and terrifying about it, as follows:

> Such a *liberated* mind stands in the midst of the All, with a joyous and confident fatalism, in the *faith* that only the individual is reprehensible, but that, in the whole, all is redeemed and affirmed— it no longer denies . . . yet such a faith is highest of all possible faiths; I have baptized it in the name of *Dionysos*.[39]

Thus, Nietzsche does not hesitate to annex Goethe to his own belief in the "Dionysian."

In Nietzsche's view, the Dionysian is the ecstatic aspect of the Greek soul. He defines it in a posthumous fragment:

> An impulse toward unity, a transcendence of the person . . . an ecstatic yes to the overall character of life . . . the great pantheistic sympathy, in joy and pain, which approves and sanctifies even the most terrible and dubious properties of life, out of an eternal will to procreation, fecundity, and eternity: a unitary feeling of the necessity of creating and destroying.[40]

Here, I have mentioned only the features that are present in Goethe and justify his annexation to the Dionysian: the tendency to unity, pantheistic sympathy, and the acceptance of the most terrible aspects of life. Goethe heralds Nietzsche, and Nietzsche was well aware of it:

> Suppose we say yes to a single, unique instant: we will thereby have said yes not only to ourselves, but to all of existence. For nothing is

for itself, either in ourselves, or in things. And if, even once, happiness has made our soul vibrate and resonate like a musical string, all the eternities were necessary to create the conditions for this Unique Event, and all eternity has been approved, redeemed, justified, affirmed, in that unique instant in which we have said yes.[41]

Not only do we find here, as in Nietzsche's praise of Goethe, which we have quoted, the idea that everything is "redeemed and affirmed" from an overall perspective, but above all, we can perceive an echo of Goethe's famous text:

What good is all this extravagance of suns, planets, and moons, of stars . . . if finally one happy person does not rejoice unconsciously at her own existence?[42]

One may ask: Why was it so important for Nietzsche that all eternity should be approved, redeemed, justified, and affirmed? All eternity is what it is, one might object, and that's that. But shouldn't we see here an answer to Goethe's "what good" is it?[43] For Nietzsche, as for Goethe, what gives meaning to the universe from the viewpoint of mankind is their "Yes" to the slightest instant of the universe, with each instant presupposing all eternities, the totality of the world or worlds.

For Nietzsche, this Dionysian faith is identified with what he calls *amor fati*, the love of fate:

My formula for greatness in man is *amor fati*: that one wishes to have nothing else than what is, either ahead or behind, or for all eternity. Not to merely put up with what is necessary, even less to conceal it—all idealism is hypocrisy in the face of what is necessary—but to love it.[44]

The Dionysian attitude, *amor fati*, can also be expressed by the doctrine of the eternal return of each instant, which, if one accepts

this myth, implies that one must will that each instant, whether it
brings us joy or pain, should be repeated eternally, and that one must
will and love that which is:

> Highest star of Being!
> Which no desire achieves
> Which no negation sullies
> Eternal Yes of Being
> Eternally, I am your Yes
> For I love you, O Eternity![45]

Nietzsche's personal fate was atrocious suffering due to his illness,
which he knew might destroy his brain.[46] It must be admitted that for
him, loving "that which is" was a heroic act. He makes a confession
on this subject, when he writes:

> I have often wondered if I did not owe more to the hardest years
> of my life than to any other. My most intimate being teaches me
> this: all that is necessary, seen from above and in the sense of a
> *great* economy, is also what is useful in itself. We must not merely
> put up with it: we must *love* it . . . *Amor fati*, that is the basis of my
> nature.[47]

Nietzsche continues by pointing out all that he owes to the
long illness that has been eroding his health: "To it I also owe my
philosophy."
      In both Nietzsche and Goethe, this love of life, including what
may be painful, even atrocious about it, is strongly inspired by Stoic
philosophy. Goethe had read Marcus Aurelius, and Nietzsche had
read both Epictetus and Marcus Aurelius, whose moralism he did
not, moreover, appreciate. This does not mean that they absolutely
required these readings to construct their attitude to fate; nevertheless, one cannot help but recognize the close kinship between this
attitude and that of the Stoics. For instance, as far as joyful consent

is concerned, how can one fail to recall this meditation by Marcus Aurelius:

> What is proper to the good person is to love and greet with joy all the events that come to meet him, and are woven together with him by Fate.[48]

Likewise, we also find the Nietzschean link between the inevitable and the useful in these phrases by Marcus Aurelius: "Everything that happens to the individual is useful to the All";[49] "What is useful to the universe is always beautiful and in season."[50] In addition, Marcus Aurelius does not hesitate to proclaim that all that is connected to natural processes in one way or another, even if it is terrible or repulsive—the gaping jaws of wild beasts, thorns, mud, old age—receives its beauty from its relation with the course of universal Nature.[51] One may also add that Nietzsche himself cites with feeling these verses from the Stoic Cleanthes, which end Epictetus's *Manual*:

> Fate, I obey you! Even if I did not want to,
> I would have to, although amid sighs![52]

However, there is a huge difference between Goethe and Nietzsche; for Goethe's joyous fatalism, of which Nietzsche speaks, is inspired not only by Stoicism but also, after his discovery of Eastern and Persian literature, by Islam. As he writes in the *West-Eastern Divan*, completed in 1815:

> It is foolish that each, in his case,
> Values his particular opinion.
> If "Islam" means "submitting to God,"
> We all live and die in Islam.[53]

Goethe loves to take up this formulation "we all live in Islam," for instance in a letter of September 19, 1831, to Adèle Schopenhauer, with regard to a cholera epidemic.[54] There is indisputably a belief in providence in the old Goethe.[55] Yet Goethe's God-providence is not a personal God, like Allah, but is identified with Nature; he is a God who is immanent within the All. From this viewpoint, Goethe is not that far from Nietzsche, who justifies the most atrocious aspects of existence by replacing them within an "overall perspective," appealing to the "great pantheistic sympathy in joy and in pain."

In any case, there is in Goethe, as in Nietzsche, an important divergence from Stoicism and Islam. For the Stoics, consent to the world is a purely ethical act, a choice of the faculty of judgment. For Goethe and Nietzsche, this ethical choice presupposes an aesthetic kind of activity (which is excluded by Muḥammad).[56] It is in art and through art that one can accede to the consent to existence and that one can say "yes" to life. For Goethe and Nietzsche, art is a privileged means of access to reality, a mode of knowledge that leads its practitioner to feel what Nietzsche calls the Dionysian experience. In this, Goethe and Nietzsche are the heirs of Alexander Baumgarten, the founder of aesthetics, who in 1750 affirmed in his *Aesthetica* that there is an aesthetic truth in addition to logical truth. For instance, he contrasted an eclipse as observed by astronomers and mathematicians to an eclipse as observed with emotion by a shepherd talking about it with his beloved.[57] Aesthetic perception always contains an affective element of pleasure, admiration, or fear. This introduction of affectivity into the perception of reality, this appearance of a "feeling of existence," was to be found in Rousseau, Goethe, Schelling, all of German Romanticism, and in Nietzsche.

In Goethe and in Nietzsche, the consent to existence is linked to an aesthetic experience, but not to just any such experience. For instance, Goethe reproaches English poetry for being depressing and having inspired, in the time of his youth, a "somber disgust for life" in German youth.[58] He himself experienced this feeling very strongly, always keeping a dagger within hand's reach for this purpose. Finally, however, he came to laugh at himself and "resolved to live."[59] In order to be able to live in serenity, however, he felt the need to externalize everything he had felt in a literary work, and this was the novel *Werther*. This need to exorcise painful feelings is, one might say, rather banal. But what is very much less banal is the definition of "true" poetry that Goethe opposes to English poetry, and of which Homeric poetry and ancient poetry in general are the models, since in his view, ancient people, unlike Romantics or Christians, found their joy in earthly existence. For him, this true poetry is a "profane gospel" which brings us peace and serenity, because it lifts us up and makes us see things from up high, as if from a balloon.[60] It is always the result of an ascesis, a transformation of the gaze that resituates things within the All, within an overall perspective. Painting is also a means of acceding to the joy of existence:

> To see before oneself, all day long, the magnificence of the world, and to now feel the complete gift of representation, suddenly granted! What joy, to be able to approach what is inexpressible through lines and colors![61]

In general, the mission of art consists in "raising each person above himself."[62]

For Nietzsche as well, art is at the same time the means to say "yes" to existence and the expression of this choice. More explicitly than Goethe, however, he links art and existence closely together. As early as *The Birth of Tragedy*, he posits what he calls the first principle of his metaphysics of art: "Existence and the world can only be justified as aesthetic phenomena."[63] Almost twenty years later, he writes: "The world as a work of art engendering itself."[64] If existence has terrifying aspects, it is because ugliness and dissonance are part of the aesthetic game, whether in the art of nature or in human art. For Nietzsche, art must not express dissatisfaction in the face of the real, as Romantic or Wagnerian art does, but proclaim "gratitude before the happiness one has enjoyed,"[65] that happiness which, for Nietzsche, consists in participating, even in the midst of suffering, in the great artwork of the world. Like Raphael, one must be "grateful for existence."[66] In this perspective, art will be an "art of apotheosis," as is, Nietzsche says, the poetry of Homer. "Art is affirmation, blessing and divinization of existence."[67] We find an analogous attitude in Rilke. For him, the poet's Orphic mission is to "celebrate" earthly things and to glorify existence.[68]

Conclusion

At the end of this book, we have thus encountered once again the two major themes of *The Veil of Isis*: the two dimensions, cosmic and aesthetic, of human existence, which, in my previous book, I summarized by quoting Nietzsche: "To go beyond myself and yourself. To feel in a cosmic way"[1] and by writing that nature is art, and art, nature, since human art is merely a particular case of the art of nature.[2]

I don't pretend to affirm that the consent to being that Goethe proposes, and inherits, in part, from the Stoics and Spinoza, is the most perfect answer to the tragic problem of human existence. It is enough for me to propose a model that may or may not be suitable to any specific reader. For my part, I am seduced by this attitude of wonder. However, I have long had doubts, which I have already expressed several times. On the one hand, isn't this interior attitude reserved for the privileged? On the other, can one resign oneself to acquiescing to the immense suffering in which the majority of humanity is submerged, crushed by the appetites for power and wealth, or by the blind fanaticism of a small number of unscrupulous men?

As I complete this book, I have the feeling that I have set forth the viewpoint of a privileged person who can afford the luxury of practicing "spiritual exercises." I said to myself: we intellectuals live in a bubble, like Homunculus, and we should imitate him, by smashing our vial against the throne of Galatea. Shouldn't we, like the Stoics, admit that action, action in the service of others, is part of the philosophical life? At the same time, however, I became aware of the merit of Goethe, who was a man of action at Weimar, but who, especially, at the end of his life, gave such an important place, in all his works, to action in the service of human beings. The symbol of this orientation of Goethe's thought is the evolution of his hero Wilhelm Meister, a man of the theater who became a doctor.

One might say, moreover, that the basic intuition that inspired all of Goethe's thought consists in considering that reality, as is said in the poem "One and All," is an "eternal, living action." It is in this sense that Faust translates the first sentence of the Gospel according to John: not "In the beginning was the Word, or Discourse," but "In the beginning was Action," because only action is capable of creating.[3] What counts in Goethe's view is not to talk, but to think and to act:

To think and to act, that is the summit of all wisdom . . . Both must eternally alternate in their effect on life, like inhalation and exhalation . . . Action must be tested by thought, and thought by action.[4]

The philosophical life consists not merely in talking and writing, but in communal and social action. This was already the opinion of Epictetus and Marcus Aurelius. It is also in this perspective of action that we must understand the Goethean maxim that we have adopted as the title of the book, "Don't forget to live," by which we wished to summarize the extraordinary love of life that can be observed in Goethe.

This maxim is the translation of *Memento vivere*, which Goethe opposes to *Memento mori*: "Don't forget to die!," "Think about death." This latter maxim means that one must think about a future event in order to prepare oneself for it. The *Memento vivere* is not symmetrical to the *Memento mori*, and it is a paradoxical motto. Is it possible to forget that one is alive, since, precisely, one is alive? And yet, as early the fifth century BCE, Antiphon the Sophist, as we have seen, reproached his contemporaries with forgetting the present life, while preparing for another life.[5] In the Renaissance, Montaigne writes these lines, which I have always admired:

> "I haven't done a thing today."—"Why! Have you not lived? That is not only the most basic of your employments, it is the most glorious." . . . Our most great and glorious achievement is to live our life fittingly . . . It is an accomplishment, absolute and as it were God-like, to know how to enjoy our being as we ought.[6]

Here too, a human being has forgotten that he is alive, by allowing himself to become absorbed by one of life's details. These two viewpoints, of Antiphon and of Montaigne, introduce us to the two meanings that can be given to Goethe's maxim.

First of all, for Goethe, to live is to be active, to act in the present. "Don't forget to live" then means: "Do not forget your daily task, the action you must accomplish in the service of human beings: in a word, your duty."

Yet "don't forget to live" can also mean "don't forget to enjoy life." For Goethe, enjoying life means, first and foremost, to fully enjoy the pleasures of life; and it must be admitted that, led by Christiane, he appreciated, perhaps a bit too much, not only the pleasures of love but also those of food and drink. However, for him, enjoying life also meant finding his joy in existence itself, in what is marvelous in the activity of body and of mind. Finally, it means sharing in the joy that the "eternal, living action," in which "we have life, movement, and being," finds in its activity.[7]

Translator's Note

For Greek and Latin texts other than Marcus Aurelius, I have usually cited the English translations from the Loeb Classical Library (https://www.hup.harvard.edu/collection.php?cpk=1031), which I have sometimes modified. In the case of Marcus, I have translated Hadot's French version, which I then compared against the original Greek.

With regard to texts from Goethe, I have initially made a literal translation from Hadot's French translation, then compared the result against the original German (almost all Goethe's works, except for some of his correspondence, can be consulted here: http://www.zeno.org/Literatur/M/Goethe,+Johann+Wolfgang). In some cases, this procedure led to results that diverge from the French translations Hadot used. The translations of passages from Goethe's works, especially his poetry, make no claim to literary merit: my top priority has been to remain as close to the original as possible. Unless otherwise indicated, square brackets [. . .] indicate my additions. In addition to the list of editions and translations Hadot used, I have consulted the following:

Goethe, Johann Wolfgang von. *Conversations with Eckermann, 1823–1832.* Trans. John Oxenford. San Francisco: North Point Press, 1984.

_____. *Goethes Gespräche*. In *Gesamtausgabe*, ed. Flodoard Frhr. von Biedermann et al. 5 vols. Leipzig: F. W. v. Biedermann, 1909–11.

_____. *Maxims and Reflections*. Trans. Elisabeth Stopp. Ed. Peter Hutchinson. London: Penguin Books, 1998.

_____. *Wilhelm Meister's Apprenticeship*. Ed. and trans. Eric A. Blackall in cooperation with Victor Lange. New York: Suhrkamp, 1989. (*Goethe's Collected Works*, vol. 9.)

_____. *Wilhelm Meister's Journeyman Years, or The Renunciants*. Trans. Jan van Heurck and Krishna Winston. Ed. Jane K. Brown. Princeton, NJ: Princeton University Press, 1995. (*Goethe's Collected Works*, vol. 10.)

Hölderlin, Friedrich. *Selected Poems and Fragments*. Trans. Michael Hamburger. Ed. Jeremy Adler. London: Penguin, 1998.

Nietzsche, Friedrich. *Sämtliche Werke. Kritische Studienausgabe* (KSA), ed. Giorgio Colli and Mazzino Montinari. 15 vols. Berlin: De Gruyter, 1988.

Notes

Foreword

1. This quotation from Goethe's *Conversations with Eckermann* closes Pierre Hadot's seminal essay "Spiritual Exercises," in *Philosophy as a Way of Life: Spiritual Exercises from Socrates to Foucault* (1993), ed. A. I. Davidson, trans. M. Chase (Malden, MA, 1995), 109, translation modified.

2. Hadot, *Philosophy as a Way of Life*; Hadot, *What Is Ancient Philosophy?* (1995), trans. M. Chase (Cambridge, MA, 2002).

3. For some important biographical details about Hadot's interest in Goethe, see Ilsetraut Hadot, "L'idéalisme allemande a-t-il, chez Pierre Hadot, perverti la compréhension de la philosophie antique?," *Revue des Études Grecques* 129, no. 1 (2016): 209–10.

4. Richard Rorty, "Keeping Philosophy Pure: An Essay on Wittgenstein" (1976), in *Consequences of Pragmatism (Essays, 1972–1980)* (Minneapolis, 1982), 19.

5. Cf. below, p. 000, translation modified.

6. Pierre Hadot, *The Present Alone Is Our Happiness: Conversations with Jeannie Carlier and Arnold I. Davidson* (2001), trans. M. Djaballah (Stanford, CA, 2009), 140, translation modified. Hadot even claims that his choice of the expression "spiritual exercises" was influenced by the title of a 1942 special issue of the literary journal *Fontaine*, "On Poetry as Spiritual Exercise" (ibid., 92).

Preface

1. "'Le présent seul est notre bonheur': La valeur de l'instant présent chez Goethe et dans la philosophie antique," *Diogène*, no. 133 (January–March

1986): 56–81; "La Terre vue d'en haut et le voyage cosmique. Le point de vue d'en haut et le voyage cosmique. Le point de vue du poète, du philosophe et de l'historien," in J. Schneider and Léger-Orine, eds., *Frontières en conquêtes spatiales* (Dordrecht, 1988), 31–40; "Der Blick von oben," in P. Hadot, *Philosophie als Lebensform* (Berlin, 1995), 123–35; "Emblèmes et symboles goethéens. Du caducée d'Hermès à la plante archétype," in *L'Art des confins, Mélanges offerts à Maurice de Gandillac* (Paris, 1985), 438–44.

2. See below, p. 75.

3. [Goethe, *Wilhelm Meister's Apprenticeship*, ed. and trans. Eric A. Blackall (New York, 1989), 331 (8.5).]

4. In H. Fuhrmann et al., eds., *Wilhelm Meister und seine Nachfahren* (Cassel, 2000), 33–52.

Chapter 1

1. *Goethes Gespräche*, 1:232 (interview with Friederike Brun in Karlsbad, July 9, 1795).

2. *Faust II*, act 3, ll.9381–82.

3. *Faust II*, act 1, l.4685.

4. *Faust II*, act 1, ll.6487–500.

5. *Faust II*, act 3, ll.9370–71.

6. *Faust II*, act 3, l.9419.

7. *Faust II*, act 3, ll.9377–84.

8. *West-Eastern Divan, Book of Suleika*: "They say that Bahram Gur invented rhyme" [see BA, 3:104; trans. Ormsby, 148–49]. See also *West-Eastern Divan, Book of Paradise, Remembrance*, trans. Lichtenberger, 284–85.

9. *Faust II*, act 3, ll.9411–18.

10. *Marienbad Elegy*, 2nd stanza. [See BA, 1:497.]

11. D. Lohmeyer, *Faust und die Welt. Der zweite Teil der Dichtung. Eine Anleitung zum Lesen des Textes* (Munich, 1975), 327.

12. S. Morenz, *Die Zauberflöte* (Münster, 1952), 89.

13. Goethe to Zelter, October 19, 1829, in *Goethes Briefe*, HA, 4:346.

14. In the text just cited, Goethe uses the word *trivial* in German, but in general the trivial, the banal, etc., are designated by *das Gemeine*.

15. Goethe, *Epilogue to Schiller's Bell*, 4th stanza [see Goethe, BA, 2:92]. I do not think that *das Gemeine* can be translated by "the banal course of things," as R. Ayrault does. In my view, it is not things that achieve mastery over us, but a certain psychological and moral state brought about by habit, routine, and social conventions, which prevent us from seeing what is ideal.

16. Goethe, *Wilhelm Meister's Journeyman Years*, 2.1 [HA, 8:156, 205], cited by E. Bertram, *Nietzsche. Essai de Mythologie*, trans. P. Pitrou (Paris, 1990), 437.

17. Goethe, *Maxims and Reflections*, HA, 12:512, nos. 1041–43.

18. On the worries that "darken the entire universe," see Goethe, *Journeyman Years*, 1.10.

19. *Conversations with Eckermann*, April 10, 1829 [*Goethes Gespräche*, in *Gesamtausgabe*, ed. Flodoard Frhr. Von Biedermann et al., 5 vols. (Leipzig, 1909–11), 4:100, no. 2278].

20. Interview with Riemer, August 28, 1808, cited by W. Schadewaldt, *Goethestudien. Natur und Altertum* (Zürich, 1963), 211, 221.

21. *Goethes Briefe*, HA, 4:346–47.

22. Goethe to Sickler, April 23, 1812, in *Goethes Briefe*, HA, 3:184. On the notion of *kairos*, cf. M. Jaeger, "Kairos und Chronos—oder: Der prägnante Moment ist flüchtig. Antike Philosophie, klassische Lebenskunstlehre und moderne Verzweiflung," in *Prägnanter Moment. Studien zur deutsche Literatur der Aufklärung und Klassik, Festschrift für Hans-Jürgen Schings* (Wurzburg, 2002), 405–20.

23. Goethe, *On the Laocoon*, HA, 12:59.

24. On this theme, see F. Bremer, *Die Wahl des Augenblicks in der griechischen Kunst* (Munich, 1969).

25. Goethe, *Journey to Italy*, Verona, September 16, 1786 [HA, 11:41–42].

26. Goethe, *Journey to Italy*, Naples, May 17, 1787 [HA, 11:322].

27. *Faust II*, act 3, ll.9518–19.

28. Cf. the commentary by E. Trunz, HA, 3:547.

29. *Faust II*, act 3, ll.9562–65.

30. Ibid., ll.9550–53.

31. Schiller, *The Gods of Greece*, 6. Cf. P. Hadot, *The Veil of Isis: An Essay on the History of the Idea of Nature* (Cambridge, MA, 2006), 81–86.

32. Schiller, *Gods of Greece*, 16.

33. Hölderlin, *The Archipelago* [Friedrich Hölderlin, *Sämtliche Werke. Kleine Stuttgarter Ausgabe*, vol. 2, ed. Friedrich Beissner (Stuttgart, 1953), 114 [Friedrich Hölderlin, *Selected Poems and Fragments*, trans. Michael Hamburger, ed. Jeremy Adler (London, 1998), 212].

34. Goethe, *Winckelmann*, HA, 12:98–99.

35. Ibid., 99.

36. Plotinus, *Enneads*, 1.4 (46), 1.10.

37. K. Schneider, *Die schweigenden Götter* (Hildesheim, 1966), 6.

38. Ch. Andler, *Nietzsche. Sa vie et sa pensée* (Paris, 1958), 1:195. See the work by G. Billeter, *Die Anschauungen vom Wesen des Griechentums* (Leipzig, 1911), especially 133–45.

39. A. Boeckh, *Die Staatshaushaltung der Athener* (1817), 2:159.

40. A. Schopenhauer, *The World as Will and Representation* [Arthur Schopenhauer, *Zürcher Ausgabe. Werke in zehn Bänden* (Zürich, 1977), 4:686, citing Theognis, 425–28].

41. Cf. Ch. Andler, *Nietzsche. Sa vie et sa pensée*, 1:195–96. On Nietzsche's complex attitude to this question, see my preface to E. Bertram, *Nietzsche. Essai de mythologie*, French trans. P. Pitrou (1990), 8 and 30. [See Hadot, "Introduction to Ernst Bertram, Nietzsche: attempt at a mythology," trans. Paul Bishop, *The Agonist* 3, no. 1 (March 2010), http://www.nietzschecircle.com/AGONIST/2010_03/translationHadot.html.]

42. Hesiod, *Works and Days*, ll.95–106. On this pessimism, cf. A.-J. Festugière, *Idéal religieux des grecs et l'Évangile* (Paris, 1932), 161ff.; the translations from Solon and Sophocles that follow are based on this work.

43. Hesiod, *Works and Days*, ll.176–78.

44. Solon, frag. 14. [The French original erroneously indicates fr. 114. See *Tyrtaeus, Solon, Theognis, Mimnermus, Greek Elegiac Poetry: From the Seventh to the Fifth Centuries BC*, ed. and trans. D. Gerber (Cambridge, MA, 1999), 136.]

45. Sophocles, *Oedipus the King*, l.1186. [Trans. Hugh Lloyd-Jones in Sophocles, *Ajax. Electra. Oedipus Tyrannus* (Cambridge, MA, 1994), 453.]

46. Horace, *Odes*, 3, 1, 40 [Horace, *Odes and Epodes*, ed. and trans. Niall Rudd (Cambridge, MA, 2004), 142–43].

47. Lucretius, *On Nature*, 3.1053ff. [Lucretius, *On the Nature of Things*, trans. W. H. D. Rouse, rev. Martin F. Smith (Cambridge, MA, 1924), 273].

48. On this subject, cf. J. Pigeaud, *La maladie de l'âme: Étude sur la relation de l'âme et du corps dans la tradition médico-philosophique antique*, 2nd ed. (1981; Paris, 1989).

49. Seneca, *On Peace of Mind*, 2.6–15.

50. Goethe, *Winckelmann*, HA, 12:100–101.

51. P. Hadot, *Le Voile d'Isis*, 285ff. [Hadot, *Veil of Isis*, 292ff.].

52. Diogenes Laertius, *Lives and Doctrines of Illustrious Philosophers*, 1.77.

53. Antiphon the Sophist, in *Les présocratiques*, ed. P. Dumont (Paris, 1981), 1112 [= fr. 53a Diels-Kranz, fr. D53 and D48 in *Early Greek Philosophy*, vol. 9: *Sophists*, part 2, ed. and trans. André Laks and Glenn W. Most (Cambridge, MA, 2016), 73, 69].

54. Diogenes Laertius, *Lives and Doctrines of the Illustrious Philosophers*, 2.66 [Diogenes Laertius, *Lives of Eminent Philosophers*, vol. 1, trans. R. D. Hicks (Cambridge, MA, 1925), 194].

55. Athenaeus, *Deipnosophists*, 13.544a–b [Athenaeus, *The Learned Banqueters*, vol. 6, ed. and trans. S. Douglas Olson (Cambridge, MA, 2010)].

56. Cicero, *On the Extreme Terms of Goods and Evils*, 1.18, 59.

57. Ibid., 1.18, 60 [Cicero, *On Ends*, trans. H. Rackham (Cambridge, MA, 1914), 63, modified].

58. Seneca, *Letters to Lucilius*, 15.9. [Seneca, *Epistles*, vol. 1: *Epistles 1–65*, trans. Richard M. Gummere (Cambridge, MA, 1917), 100, modified.]

59. Greek text and Italian translation in G. Arrighetti, *Epicuro, Opere* (Turin, 1973), 567, fr. 240 [fr. 469].

60. Cicero, *On the Extreme Terms of Goods and Evils*, 1.18.6 [Cicero, *On Ends*, trans. Rackham, 66, modified].

61. Cf. Aristotle, *Nicomachean Ethics*, 10.3.1174a, lines 17ff. Cf. H.-J. Krämer, *Platonismus und hellenistische Philosophie* (Berlin, 1973), 188ff.

62. Horace, *Odes*, 2.16, 25 [Horace, *Odes and Epodes*, ed. and trans. Rudd, 128, modified].

63. *Vatican Sentences*, 14, in *Épicure, Lettres, maximes, sentences*, trans. J.-Fr. Balaudé (whose translation is slightly different from mine) (Paris, 1994), 210.

64. Horace, *Odes*, 1.11.7–8 [Horace, *Odes and Epodes*, ed. and trans. Rudd, p. 44–45, modified].

65. Horace, *Epistles*, 1.4.13–14 [Horace, *Satires, Epistles, The Art of Poetry*, trans. H. Rushton Fairclough (Cambridge, MA, 1926), 246–47, modified].

66. Lucretius, *On Nature*, 3.1034–35 [Lucretius, *On the Nature of Things*, trans. Rouse, 174–75, modified].

67. Horace, *Odes*, 3.29, 41–43 [Horace, *Odes and Epodes*, ed. and trans. Rudd, 214–15].

68. Lucretius, *On Nature*, 3.16–17.

69. *Vatican Sentences*, §10, in *Épicure, Lettres, maximes, sentences*, trans. J.-Fr. Balaudé (Paris, 1994), 219 (see the note by J.-Fr. Balaudé).

70. L. Robin, *Lucrèce, De la Nature, Commentaire des Livres III–IV* (1926; Paris, 1962), 151.

71. Marcus Aurelius, *Writings for Himself*, 9.6.

72. Ibid., 7.29.3, 3.12.1.

73. Cf. P. Hadot, *La Citadelle intérieure* (Paris, 1997), 152–54 [Hadot, *The Inner Citadel* (Cambridge, MA, 1998), 135–37].

74. Marcus Aurelius, *Writings for Himself*, 12.3.3–4.

75. Seneca, *Letters to Lucilius*, 78.14 [for a different translation, cf. Seneca, *Epistles*, vol. 2: *Epistles 66–92*, trans. Richard M. Gummere (Cambridge, MA, 1920), 191]. See also Seneca, *On Benefits*, 2.2.4–5 [Seneca, *Moral Essays*, vol. 3: *De Beneficiis*, trans. John W. Basore (Cambridge, MA, 1935), 460, modified].

76. Seneca, *Letters to Lucilius*, 74.27.

77. Plutarch, *On Common Notions against the Stoics*, §8, 1062a [Plutarch, *Moralia*, vol. 13, pt. 2: *Stoic Essays*, trans. Harold Cherniss (Cambridge, MA, 1976), 683, modified].

78. Marcus Aurelius, *Writings for Himself*, 2.5.2 and 7.69.

79. Seneca, *Letters to Lucilius*, 101.10. [For a different translation, cf. Seneca, *Epistles*, vol. 3: *Epistles 93–124*, trans. Richard M. Gummere (Cambridge, MA, 1925), 163.]

80. Marcus Aurelius, *Writings for Himself*, 2.14.3.

81. Seneca, *On Benefits*, 7.3.3.

82. Plutarch, *On Common Notions*, §27, 1078.

83. Marcus Aurelius, *Writings for Himself*, 6.37.

84. Ibid, 10.5.

85. Ibid., 10. 21.

86. Seneca, *Letters to Lucilius*, 66.6.

87. Conversation with J. D. Falk, in *Goethes Gespräche*, ed. Biedermann, 4:469.

88. On this very important movement of ideas, cf. Ph. Benk and D. Thouard, eds., *Popularité de la philosophie* (Paris, 1995).

89. "Betrachtung der Zeit," in A. Gryphius, *Gedichte. Eine Auswahl*, ed. Adalbert Elschenbroich (Stuttgart, 1968), 106. This text was very kindly pointed out to me by my dear colleague Klaus Schöpsdau, Professor at the University of Saarbrück. [The bracketed addition is Hadot's.]

90. J.-J. Rousseau, *Rêveries du promeneur solitaire* (Paris, 1964), 101–2.

91. Ibid., 103.

92. Cf. above, pp. 3 and 8–9.

93. Schadewaldt, *Goethestudien*, 476n103. On the uses of the word *Gegenwart* in Goethe, cf. J. Krause, "Wort und Begriff "Gegenwart" bei Goethe," PhD diss., Humboldt-Universität, Berlin (typescript).

94. *Voyage in Italy*, Verona, September 16, 1786 [HA, 11:41].

95. Goethe, *Marienbad Elegy*, in *Poésies*, 2:679 [Goethe, BA, *Poetische Werke*, 1:500].

96. Cf. above, p. 21.

97. Cf. the study by Schadewaldt, *Goethestudien*, 433–58, from which I borrow several examples in what follows.

98. *Faust II*, act 3, l. 9413: "my words falter."

99. "An Grafen Paar," in *Goethes sämtliche Werke*, JA, 3:12 [Goethe, BA, *Poetische Werke*, 1:727]. On this theme, cf. B. Hillebrand, "'Der Augenblick ist Ewigkeit.' Goethes wohltemperierte Verhältnis zur Zeit," *Akademie der Wissenschaft und der Literatur*, Mainz-Stuttgart, 1997.

100. *Faust II*, act 3, ll.9381–82.

101. On this theme, see W. Emrich, *Die Symbolik von Faust II* (Bonn, 1964), 343, and D. Lohmeyer, *Faust und die Welt*, 321.

102. *West-Eastern Divan*, HA, 2:70.

103. In HA, 2:631. See also J. Müller, "Goethes Zeiterlebnis im 'West-östlichen Divan,'" in *Gestaltung Umgestaltung, Festschrift zum 75. Geburtstag von Hermann August Korff*, ed. J. Müller, Leipzig, 1957, 155.

104. I. B. Pasternak, *Le Docteur Jivago* (Paris, 1958), 639 [Pasternak, *Doctor Zhivago* (New York, 1958), 414].

105. *West-Eastern Divan* [Goethe: BA, *Poetische Werke*, 3:108–9]. On this poem, see the commentaries by H. Lichtenberger, 466; by E. Trunz, HA, 2:642; and by J. Müller, "Goethes Zeiterlebnis im 'West-östlichen Divan,'" 157.

106. W. Emrich, *Die Symbolik von Faust II*, 343–44.

107. Cf. A. Schöne, *J.-W. Goethe, Faust, Kommentare* (Darmstadt, 1999), 582–87.

108. HA, 3:668–69.

109. For this last hypothesis, cf. H.-J. Weigand, "Wetten und Pakt in Goethes Faust," in *Aufsätze zu Goethes Faust I*, ed. W. Keller (Darmstadt, 1984), 426–27.

110. *Entretiens avec le chancelier de Müller*, French trans. A. Béguin (Paris, 1931), 285.

111. See W. Schadewaldt, *Goethestudien*, 203, 246.

112. *Faust I*, ll.3188–92, as cited by Schadewaldt, *Goethestudien*, 137.

113. *Faust II*, act 5, ll.11581–86, as cited by Schadewaldt, *Goethestudien*, 1321–22.

114. Cf. *Marienbad Elegy*, l.100, cited below.

115. Marcus Aurelius, *Writings for Himself*, 6.5.

116. HA, 1:307.

117. Goethe, *Conversations with Chancellor Von Müller*, November 4, 1823 [*Goethes Gespräche*, ed. Biedermann, 3:78, no. 2185].

118. Goethe, *Egmont*, act 2 [HA, 4:398].

119. Goethe, *Conversations with the Chancellor von Müller*, September 7, 1827 [*Goethes Gespräche*, ed. Biedermann, 3:439, no. 2539].

120. Goethe, *Lebensregel* [Rule of Life], HA, 1:319.

121. Marcus Aurelius, *Writings for Himself,* 13.1–2

122. *Marienbad Elegy,* ll.91–102, HA, 1:384.

123. *Conversations with Eckermann,* February 28, 1831 [Goethe, *Gedenkausgabe der Werke, Briefe und Gespräche,* ed. E. Beutler, vol. 24: *Johann Peter Eckermann, Gespräche mit Goethe in den letzten Jahren seines Lebens* (Zürich, 1948), 468].

124. [Goethe, *Marienbad Elegy,* ll.92–97.]

125. *Conversations with Eckermann,* February 28, 1823 [66–67, ed. Beutler].

126. *Voyage in Italy,* Rome, October 27, 1827 [HA, 11:418].

127. Cf. above, p. 24.

128. *Poetry and Truth,* book 3, p. 14 [HA, 10:31].

129. Cf. above, pp. 24–25.

130. Goethe to Auguste von Bernstoff, April 17, 1823, *Goethes Briefe,* HA, 4:63.

131. "Vermächtnis" (Legacy) [BA, *Poetische Werke,* 1:541–42].

132. *West-Eastern Divan* [BA, *Poetische Werke,* 3:54–55].

133. *Maximen und Reflexionen,* §752, HA, 12:471 (§314 Hecker).

134. *Faust II,* act 4, ll.12014–105.

135. "Vermächtnis" (Legacy), l.3.

136. *Poetry and Truth,* book 8 [HA, 9:353].

137. *One and All* [BA, *Poetische Werke,* 1:540].

138. *Blessed Nostalgia,* in *West-Eastern Divan* [BA, *Poetische Werke,* 3:21].

139. See above, p. 45.

140. *Maximen und Reflexionen,* §1088, HA, 12:518.

141. *West-Eastern Divan, Book of the Parsi* [BA, 3:139].

Chapter 2

1. German text in HA, 13:255–56.

2. B. Saint Girons, *Le Sublime de l'Antiquité à nos jours* (Paris, 2005), 96.

3. We find the image of a mountain as an altar in the poem "Winter Journey in the Harz" [BA, 1:317].

4. H. Blumenberg, *Die Legitimität der Neuzeit* (Frankfurt, 1966), 336n247 [Blumenberg, *The Legitimacy of the Modern Age,* trans. R. M. Wallace (Cambridge, MA, 1985), 341].

5. J. Burckhardt, *Griechische Kulturgeschichte,* 2:2, in *Gesammelte Werke,* 6: 82. There is a critique of Burckhardt's opinion in G. Pochat, *Figur und*

Landschaft. Eine historische Interpretation der Landschaftsmalerei (Berlin, 1973), 182ff.

6. On the feelings that mountains inspire in modern mankind, cf. M. H. Nicholson, *Mountain Gloom and Mountain Glory: The Development of the Aesthetics of the Infinite* (Ithaca, NY, 1959).

7. J. Le Goff, *La Naissance du Purgatoire* (Paris, 1981), 11.

8. Homer, *Iliad*, 4.275–76.

9. Ibid., 5.770–72 [*The Iliad of Homer*, trans. R. Lattimore (Chicago, 1951)].

10. Apollonius of Rhodes, *Argonautica*, 1.1112–16 [Apollonius Rhodius, *Argonautica*, ed. and trans. William H. Race (Cambridge, MA, 2009), 93].

11. On the view from above and geography, see the pages on this subject by Chr. Jacob, *La description de la terre habitée de Denys d'Alexandrie ou La leçon de géographie* (Paris, 1990), 23–28.

12. [Or "watchtowers" (*skopias*).]

13. Aristophanes, *Clouds*, ll.275–90 [translation, slightly modified, from Aristophanes, *Clouds. Wasps. Peace*, ed. and trans. Jeffrey Henderson (Cambridge, MA, 1998)].

14. Seneca, *Letters to Lucilius*, 89.21; Martial, *Epigrams*, 4.45: Pliny the Younger, *Letters*, 5.6 and 2.17; Statius, *Silvae*, 2.2; *Palatine Anthology*, 9. 808.

15. Seneca, *Letters to Lucilius*, 79.2.

16. *Historia Augusta, Life of Hadrian*, 13.3.

17. Ibid., 14.3.

18. Ammianus Marcellinus, *Histories*, 22.14.4–6 [Ammianus Marcellinus, *History*, trans. J. C. Rolfe (Cambridge, MA, 1940), 2.20–26].

19. Lucretius, *On Nature*, 6.468–69, 6.421–22 [Lucretius, *On the Nature of Things*, trans. Rouse].

20. Diodorus Siculus, *Historical Library*, 17.7.6.

21. Apollonius of Rhodes, *Argonautics*, 3.154–84 [Apollonius Rhodius, *Argonautica*, ed. and trans. William H. Race (Cambridge, MA, 2009)].

22. A.-J. Festugière, *La Révélation d'Hermès Trismégiste*, 2: 445n6. Pp. 441–59 are very interesting for the problem that concerns us here.

23. Ibid., 445n6.

24. Fr. Frontisi-Ducroux, *Dédale. Mythologie de l'artisan dans la Grèce antique* (1975; Paris, 2000).

25. For some historians, the depiction of the flight of the mind raises the question of a possible influence of shamanism. I have discussed this question in *Qu'est-ce que la philosophie antique?* (Paris, 1995), 276–89

[Hadot, *What Is Ancient Philosophy?* (Cambridge, MA, 2002, 181–206], and in the article "Shamanism and Greek Philosophy," in H.-P. Frankfort and R. Hamayon, eds., *The Concept of Shamanism: Uses and Abuses* (Budapest, 2002), 385–402.

26. *On the Sublime*, 35.2–3 [Aristotle, Longinus, Demetrius, *Poetics. Longinus: On the Sublime. Demetrius: On Style*, trans. Stephen Halliwell, W. Hamilton Fyfe, Doreen C. Innes, and W. Rhys Roberts, rev. Donald A. Russell (Cambridge, MA, 1995)].

27. Cicero, *Republic*, 6.9–29.

28. Philo, *De specialibius Legibus*, 3.1–2 [translation, modified, after Philo, *On the Decalogue. On the Special Laws, Books 1–3*, trans. F. H. Colson (Cambridge, MA, 1937)]. Compare 2, § 644, on wise men as citizens of the world.

29. Cicero, *On the Nature of the Gods*, 1.21.54 [Cicero, *On the Nature of the Gods. Academics*, trans. H. Rackham (Cambridge, MA)].

30. Lucretius, *On Nature*, 1.72–74, 2.1044–47, 3.16–17 [Lucretius, *On the Nature of Things*, trans. Rouse].

31. Seneca, *Letters to Lucilius*, 102.21 [Seneca, *Epistles*, vol. 3: *Epistles 93–124*, trans. Richard M. Gummere (Cambridge, MA, 1925)].

32. Marcus Aurelius, *Writings for Himself*, 11.1.

33. Cf. the texts cited in P. Hadot, *What Is Ancient Philosophy?*, 118–19.

34. Seneca, *Natural Questions*, 1, Prologue, 7 [Seneca, *Natural Questions, Volume I: Books 1–3*, trans. Thomas H. Corcoran (Cambridge, MA, 1971)].

35. Cicero, *Republic*, 6.16.16 [Cicero, *On the Republic. On the Laws*, trans. Clinton W. Keyes (Cambridge, MA, 1928)]. Cf. Seneca, *Natural Questions, Prologue*, §§ 11–12; Marcus Aurelius, *Writings for Himself*, 6.36, 11.12.

36. Ovid, *Metamorphoses*, 15.147–51 [Ovid, *Metamorphoses*, vol. 2, books 9–15, trans. Frank Justus Miller, rev. G. P. Goold (Cambridge, MA, 1916)].

37. Lucretius, *On Nature*, 2.7–10 [Lucretius, *On the Nature of Things*, trans. Rouse].

38. Seneca, *Natural Questions*, 1, Prologue, §7.

39. Marcus Aurelius, *Writings for Himself*, 8.48, 9.30, 12.24.3.

40. There is an English translation of the *Icaromenippus* and the *Charon* in the Loeb Classical Library, no. 54.

41. Lucian, *Icaromenippus*, 11, citing Homer, *Iliad*, 13.4–5.

42. Homer, *Odyssey*, 11.308.

43. Lucian, *Dialogues of the Dead*, 20, Loeb Classical Library, no. 431, vol. 7, p. 102.

44. For instance, Epictetus, *Discourses*, 3.22.24.

45. Lucian, *How One Should Write History*, §41, English trans., Loeb Classical Library, vol. 6, p. 56.

46. Ibid., §49, p. 60, citing Homer, *Iliad*, 13.4–5.

47. See below, pp. 79–80.

48. Bernard Silvester, *Cosmographie*, introduction, translation and notes by J. Lemoins, Paris, 1998. The work is also known under the title *De mundi universitate libri duo sive Macrocosmus et Microcosmus*.

49. H. Tuzet, *Le Cosmos et l'imagination* (Paris, 1989), 217.

50. On these texts, see Arthur Koestler, *The Sleepwalkers. A History of Man's Changing Vision of the Universe* (London, 1959); M. H. Nicholson, *Voyages to the Moon* (New York, 1948), and *The Breaking of the Circle* (1949); H. Tuzet, *Le Cosmos et l'imagination*, 215ff.

51. Pascal, *Pensées*, ed. L. Brunschvicq (Paris, 1971), 347–49, §72, p.; 427, §305; 428, §206 [Blaise Pascal, *Pensées and Other Writings*, trans. Honor Levi (Oxford, 1995)].

52. [About 32 kilometers, or 20 miles.]

53. [About 2 kilometers, or 1.24 miles.]

54. Voltaire, *Micromégas*, chapter 1, p. 29 (Hatier Poche) [Voltaire, *Candide and Other Stories*, trans. R. Pearson (Oxford, 1998)].

55. Id., *Zadig*, chap. 9, p. 49 (Hatier Poche) [Voltaire, *Candide and Other Stories*, trans. Pearson, 132–33].

56. André Chénier, *Œuvres complètes* (Paris, 1958), 391.

57. Cf. the excellent articles by R. Denker, "Luftfahrt auf montgolfierische Art in Goethes Dichten und Denken," *Jahrbuch der Goethe-Gesellschaft* 26 (1964): 181–98, and by M. Wenzel, "Buchholz peinigt vergebens die Lüfte. Das Luftfahrt- und Ballonmotive in Goethes naturwissenschaftlichem und dichterischem Werk," *Jahrbuch des Freien Deutschen Hochstifts* (1988): 79–112. Reading these works was a great help to me in writing the present study.

58. W. Emrich, *Die Symbolik von Faust II* (Frankfurt, 1957), 370.

59. *Faust II*, act 3, ll.9952–53.

60. [Goethe, *Wilhelm Meisters Wanderjahre*, HA, 8:7.]

61. [Ibid., 10; *Wilhelm Meister's Journeyman Years, or The Renunciants*, trans. Jan van Heurck and Krishna Winston, ed. Jane K. Brown (Princeton, NJ: Princeton University Press, 1995), 100.]

62. G. Bianquis, "Goethe et Voltaire," in *Études sur Goethe* (Paris, 1951), 98.

63. See below, p. 89.

64. [BA, 1:319–20.]

65. Goethe, *Wilhelm Meister's Journeyman Years*, I, 3 [HA, 8:30; trans. Winston/Brown, 114].

66. Kant, *Critique of the Faculty of Judgment*, II, §§ 26–28 [Immanuel Kant, *Werke in zwölf Bänden*, vol. 10 (Frankfurt am Main, 1977), 172–89; English version in Immanuel Kant, *Critique of the Power of Judgment*, ed. and trans. P. Guyer and Eric Matthews (Cambridge, UK, 2000), 134–59].

67. HA, 8:561.

68. Goethe, *Wilhelm Meister's Journeyman Years*, I, 3 [HA, 8:31; trans. Winston/Brown, 115].

69. On the notion of originary phenomena, cf. G. Bianquis, *Études sur Goethe* (Paris, 1951), 45–80; Hadot, *Veil of Isis*, 220, 254–60, 279–81.

70. M. Wenzel, "Buchholz peinigt vergebens die Lüfte," 95 [for the poem, see BA, *Poetische Werke*, 1:316–19].

71. Goethe, *Die Leiden des jungen Werthers* [HA, 6:51].

72. Goethe, *Faust 1*, ll.1092–99.

73. G. Bachelard, *L'Air et les songes* (Paris, 1992), 106–16.

74. Goethe, *Wilhelm Meister, The Years of Apprenticeship*, II, 2 [HA, 7:83.].

75. *Goethes Briefe*, HA, 2:544.

76. Goethe to Kestner, February 5, 1773, WA, vol. 4, part 2, p. 52. Cf. Schadewaldt, *Goethestudien*, 134, 155.

77. *Poetry and Truth*, part 3, book 13 [HA, 9:580]. It may be interesting to add that Goethe wrote to Charlotte von Stein that Voltaire looks at things from above, as if from a balloon, but also that he looks at them with a certain contempt (June 7, 1784, *Goethes Briefe*, HA, 1:440).

78. *Faust II*, act 3, ll.9897–902.

79. Cf. above, pp. 10–13.

80. Wenzel, "Buchholz peinigt vergebens die Lüfte," especially pp. 104–5.

81. Goethe, "In the Gloomy Charnel-House," ll.31–32, HA, 1:367.

82. *Faust II*, act 5, ll.11288–303.

83. F. Scheithauer, *Kommentar zu Goethes Faust* (Stuttgart, 1959), 292.

84. A. Schöne, *Faust, Kommentare* (Darmstadt, 1999), 728.

85. Cf. below, pp. 136–37.

86. *Weimars Jubelfest* (Weimar, 1825), 37–39.

87. Cf. P. Hadot, *Le Voile d'Isis*, 251–53 [Hadot, *Veil of Isis*, 247–49].

88. Anselme de Boot, *Symbola varia* (Amsterdam, 1686), 292.

89. Martin de Vos, *Illustration des Métamorphoses d'Ovide* (Brussels, 1607).

90. With R. Ayrault (*Poésies*, 2:730), and K. Vietor ("Goethes Altersgedichte," in K. Vietor, *Geist und Form* [Bern, 1952], 254), I retain

the version: *Blauer Berge* (blue mountains) in preference to the other versions: *Luftiger Berge* (mountains swept by the winds), or *Bunter Berge* (many-colored mountains). It is more coherent with the theory of colors that underlies the poem. In *Poetry and Truth*, HA, 9:319 (book 3, 11), Goethe, evoking a pilgrimage to Mount Saint-Odile, speaks of the blue of the Swiss mountains seen in the distance, which "attracts" him and his companions.

91. The German text and French translation (which I have sometimes taken the liberty of modifying) of the various stanzas in Goethe, *Poésies*, 2:730 [for the German text, see Goethe, *Sophienaufgabe der Werke* (1891), 4:134].

92. K. Vietor, *Geist und Form*, 154ff.

93. Goethe, *Treatise on Colors*, §§779–80 [Goethe, *Gedenkausgabe der Werke, Briefe und Gespräche*, vol. 16 (Zürich, 1948–), 210].

94. *Faust II*, act 1, l. 4247.

95. Here and in the following three paragraphs, the quotation is from Goethe, *Wilhelm Meister's Journeyman Years*, I, 10 [HA, 8:117; trans. Winston/Brown, 177].

96. Cf. Fr. Frontisi-Ducroux, *Dédale*, who considers that Daedalus's behavior "is exemplary of the just way of being, of the ethos of Greek man, of balance between audacity and respect" (156).

97. Cf. above, p. 34.

98. Nietzsche, *Œuvres philosophiques complètes*, vol. 5 (1967), 562 [Nietzsche, *Gesammelte Werke, Musarion Ausgabe*, vol. 20: *Dichtungen 1859–1888* (Munich, 1920), 89].

99. E. Trunz, in Goethe, *Werke*, HA, 8:583.

100. German text and French translation in *Poésies*, 2:730.

101. Ibid., 2:730.

102. Spinoza, *Ethics*, IV, proposition 67.

103. Goethe, *Wilhelm Meister's Apprenticeship*, 8.5 [HA, 7:539; trans. Blackall, 331.

104. *Poésies*, 2:745.

105. Kant, *Critique of the Faculty of Judgment*, §42. Cf. P. Hadot, *What Is Ancient Philosophy?*, 270; id., *Veil of Isis*, 214.

106. G. Leopardi, *Zibaldone*, 3269. I owe this reference to a kind communication by Madame Novella Bellucci.

107. Baudelaire, *Œuvres complètes*, vol. 1, ed. C. Pichois (Paris, 1975), 7–11.

108. Ibid., 839, note by C. Pichois, citing Baudelaire's essay on Wagner.

109. Letters by H. von Kleist, dating from August 4 and 31, 1806.

110. E. Renan, *Œuvres complètes*, vol. 11 (Paris, 1958), 1037.

111. *Nietzsche Contra Wagner*, Epilogue, section 1 [Friedrich Nietzsche, *Kritische Studienausgabe*, ed. G. Colli and M. Montinari, vol. 6 (Berlin, 1988), 436].

112. J. Schneider and M. Léger-Orine, eds., *Frontières et conquête spatiale* (Dordrecht, 1987).

113. A. Brahic et al., ed., *La Spatiopithèque. Vers un mutation de l'homme dans l'espace* (Paris, 1987).

114. Ibid., 176 (testimony of Wubo J. Ockels).

115. *La Terre vue du ciel*, 137 (testimony of Jean-Loup Chrétien); 80 (James Irwin); 104 (Pavel Popvich); 184 (Vitaly Sebastianov).

116. Ibid., 165 (Olev Makarov); 113 (Patrick Baudry); 116 (Vladimir Lyakov); 134 (Byron Lichtenberg).

117. *Le Spatiothèque*, 179; *La Terre vue du ciel*, 59 (Alexei Leonov); 88 (Alfred Worden); 176 (Alexander Alexandrov); 220 (Sigmund Jähn).

118. *Le Spatiothèque*, 177 (Wubo Ockels).

119. *La Terre vue du ciel*, 99.

120. Ibid., 46.

121. Ibid., 53 (Loren Acton); 177 (Piot Klimack); 200 (Andrean Nikolayev).

122. Ibid., 131 (Mohammed Ahmed Faris); 138 (Sultan ben Salman al-Saoud).

123. *Le Spatiothèque*, 181.

124. *La Terre vue du ciel*, 215–16.

Chapter 3

1. Two studies are very useful for the interpretation of the poem: Th. Buck, *Goethes Urworte. Orphisch* (Frankfurt am Main, 1996); J. Schmidt, *Goethes Altersgedicht Urworte. Orphisch* (Heidelberg, 2006).

2. My translation has been influenced by those of J. F. Angelloz (*Les Pages immortelles de Goethe*, ed. H. Carossa [Paris, 1942], 164), Roger Ayrault (*Goethe, Poésies*, 2:598), and Maurice de Gandillac (in W. Benjamin, *Œuvres choisies* [Paris, 1959], 111n2) [BA, 1:549].

3. I have translated *wie* by "in conformity with" (Gandillac translates "according to," in order to underline the astrological causality that acts on the individual's development. Cf. below, pp. 88–93.

4. In the Middle Ages, it was thought that the birth of Christ had been foretold by sibyls (women inspired by Apollo) and by the prophets of Israel.

5. *Gefällig*: the word alludes to the service, good or bad, which Tukhê renders, especially to young people, but also to every human being, and it also evokes the pleasure one can sometimes find in social contacts and the variety of events.

6. *Wandelndes . . . wandelt*: Goethe plays upon the double meaning of the verb *wandeln*, which means both "to change" and "to walk"; hence the translations "changing" and "wanders."

7. As was pointed out by E. Trunz, HA, 1:729, the opposition *hinfällig-widerfällig* corresponds to the opposition, frequent in Goethe, between *hin* and *wider*, which designates a movement that goes sometimes in one direction, sometimes in the opposite direction, as for instance *Faust I*, l.2598: "Wie sich Cupido reget und hin und wider springt" (how young Cupid stirs and then leaps to and fro). For the word I have translated by "in the opposite direction," the first editions of the poem have the reading *wiederfällig*, while modern editions bear the reading *widerfällig*. This difference can be explained by the evolution of German spelling in the course of the nineteenth century. In his commentary on the passage from Goethe we have just cited (J. W. Goethe, *Faust Kommentare* [Darmstadt, 1999], 288), A. Schöne notes that the 1828 edition features the reading *hin und wieder*, but that the meaning corresponds well to the modern spelling *wider*; otherwise it would mean that Cupid "sometimes" stirs. Hence my translation, to which one should perhaps add the following nuance pointed out by E. Trunz, in his commentary on the *Urworte*, HA, 1:723, who compares the Dutch expression *medevallen-tegenvallen*, "which is favorable to us," "which is contrary to us." I have translated "that falls," thinking of the expression "that falls well, that falls badly." My particular thanks go to my friend Herman Bonne for the information and advice he gave me with regard to this difficult passage.

8. *Öde* can be translated by "Chaos" because Goethe seems to be alluding to the passage from Hesiod (*Theogony*, l.116) and especially to the *Orphic Argonautica* (ll.14 and ll.116), which use the formula "ancient Chaos" and states that Eros was born from Chaos. But the notion of Chaos is equivalent to that of the Void (cf. the note by P. Mazon to the text of Hesiod in the edition of the Collection des Universités de France, *Hésiode, Les Travaux et les Jours*: "Chaos designates a gaping depth."

9. *Bedingung*: literally "condition," but the word in isolation does not express the deep meaning, i.e., "constraining delimitation and determination."

10. The same meaning of *Zone* occurs in the poem *Die Weltseele* (The World Soul), HA, 1:248: "Begeistert reisst euch durch die nächsten Zonen ins All": "with enthusiasm, hurl yourselves through the closest spaces, into the All."

11. Goethe uses this term several times to designate the series of centuries, both as the succession of vicissitudes, and as a fatal network of implications: cf. *Faust II*, act 5, ll.11583–84: "The trace of the days of my life / cannot vanish in the ages [*Äonen*]"; *West-Eastern Divan, Chuld Nameh, Book of Paradise, Agreement*: " Do you know how many millennia [*Äonen*] we have spent in intimate union?"; *Poetry and Truth*, book 8, HA, 8:352, l.10: "The Elohim had the choice of waiting for the time [*Äonen*] . . . when the way would be open for a new creation"; "Today and Forever" (*Heute und ewig*), in *Poésies*, 2:604–5: "The ages [*Äonen*] will sink and reign alternatively."

12. K. Borinski, "Goethes *Urworte. Orphisch*," *Philologus* 69 (1910): 2–9.

13. *Georg Zoega's Abhandlungen*, ed. F. G. Welcker (Göttingen, 1817).

14. Welcker, *Georg Zoega's Abhandlungen*, 32 ff.

15. Heraclitus, fr. 119 Diels.

16. Pierre Hadot, *Inner Citadel*, 123–24.

17. Cf. the note in A. Diès, *Platon, Les lois (Livres VII–X)*, 133.

18. Cf. *Diagoras Melius. Theodorus Cyrenaeus*, ed. M. Winiarczyk (Leipzig, 1981), 29, fr. 2.

19. Plato, *Phaedo*, 107d.

20. Id., *Republic*, X, 617e, 619e. I warmly thank Mme. Fabienne Jourdan for the very illuminating remarks which she communicated to me about this text: they have been very precious to me and have helped me to comment on it.

21. *Republic*, X, 619c.

22. Proclus, *Commentary on the Republic*, trans. Festugière, 3:249.

23. Ibid.

24. *Laws*, IX, 877I.

25. G. Ricciardelli, *Inni Orfici* (Milan, 2000), xxxi.

26. Ibid., hymn 72, ll.2–3, p. 184.

27. Vettius Valens, *Anthologiarum libri*, ed. W. Kroll (Berlin, 1908), 126 (15); 160 (5); 331 (26–27).

28. Macrobius, *Saturnalia*, 1.19.16–18. I here propose my own translation, but see also the excellent translation by Ch. Guittard, *Macrobe, Saturnales*, books 1–2 (Paris, 2004), 121 [compare the English translation in Macrobius, *Saturnalia*, vol. 1, books 1–2, ed. and trans. Robert A. Kaster (Cambridge, MA, 2011)].

29. Cf. J. Flamant, *Macrobe et le néo-platonisme latin à la fin du IVe siècle* (Leiden, 1977), 653–58.

30. Paul of Alexandria, *Elementa Apotelesmatica*, ed. E. Boer (Leipzig, 1958), 47 (13).

31. Cf. F. Boll, C. Bezold, W. Gundel, *Sternglaube und Sterndeutung* (Darmstadt, 1975), 195ff.

32. Proclus, *Commentary on the Republic*, ed. W. Kroll, 2:299 (26–28); translation based on Festugière, 3:257.

33. O. Neugebauer and H. B. Van Hoesen, *Greek Horoscopes* (Philadelphia, 1959), 44–45 (no. 188) and 65 (no. 388). On the four lots in general, cf. ibid., pp. 8–9. I thank my friend Alain Segonds for drawing my attention to these texts.

34. Vettius Valens, *Anthologiarum libri*, ed. Kroll, 200–202 (4.25).

35. *Georg Zoega's Abhandlungen*, 46; 52; K. Borinski, "Goethe's Urworte. Orphisch," 8. [The bracketed addition is Hadot's.]

36. On Hermetism and astrology, cf. A.-J. Festugière, *La Révélation d'Hermès Trismégiste*, vol. 1 (Paris, 1950), 89–186.

37. K. Borinski, "Goethe's *Urworte. Orphisch*," 5.

38. Cf. ibid.

39. Goethe to Nees von Esenbeck, May 25, 1818, in Th. Buck, *Goethes Urworte. Orphisch*, 72.

40. Goethe to Ottilie von Goethe, June 21, 1818, in Th. Buck., *Goethes Urworte. Orphisch*, 73.

41. *Poetry and Truth*, book 1, p. 13 [HA, 9:10]. On Goethe's horoscope, cf. Boll, Bezold, Gundel, *Sternglaube und Sterndeutung*, 67–72; 160–163.

42. Ch. Du Bos, *Goethe* (Paris, 1949), 29.

43. Ibid., 30.

44. Goethe, commentary on the second stanza of the *Urworte*, in *Poésies*, 2: 757.

45. See above, pp. 6–7.

46. Goethe, commentary on the first stanza of the *Urworte*, in *Poésies*, 2:755. [The bracketed addition is Hadot's.]

47. *Poetry and Truth*, book 2 [HA, 9:71].

48. A. de Saint Exupéry, *Terre des Hommes*, in *Œuvres complètes*, ed. M. Austrand and M. Quesnel (Paris, 1994), 1:285.

49. *Conversations with Eckermann*, March 12, 1828 [*Goethes Gespräche*, ed. Biedermann, 6:293–94].

50. Ch. Andler, *Nietzsche, sa vie et sa pensée*, vol. 1 (Paris, 1958), 30n1.

51. Goethe, *Voyage in Italy*, 187–89, October 9, 1786 [HA, 11:93; the French original wrongly gives the date as October 1776].

52. S. Freud, "The Dynamics of Transference" (1912) [J. Strachey et al., eds., *The Standard Edition of the Complete Psychological Works of Sigmund Freud*, vol. 12 (London, 1958), 99].

53. Goethe's commentary on the third stanza of the *Urworte*, in *Poésies*, 2:759. [The bracketed addition is Hadot's.]

54. Cf above, pp. 90–91.

55. Goethe's commentary on the third stanza of the *Urworte*, in *Poésies*, 2:759.

56. Ibid.

57. Goethe's commentary on the third stanza of the *Urworte*, in *Poésies*, 2:761.

58. For instance, Th. Buck, *Goethes Urworte. Orphisch*, 54–55.

59. Cf. below, pp. 108–12.

60. *Wilhelm Meister's Journeyman Years*, VI [HA, 7:405].

61. German Text in HA, 12: 520 (no. 1120) [Goethe, *Maxims and Reflections*, trans. Stopp, 44].

62. In Goethe, *Poésies*, 1: 367 [BA, 1:316].

63. See, for instance, the poem "Amyntas," cited infra, p. 108–9.

64. *Poetry and Truth*, book 4, p. 20, HA, 10 (Hamburg, 1948), 174–76.

65. In HA, 10:651.

66. ["sonderbare aber ungeheure." I have translated Hadot's French version, but a more accurate translation might be "exceptional but monstrous."]

67. There is a long study on this theme in H. Blumenberg, *Arbeit am Mythos* (Frankfurt, 1979), 435–604 [Blumenberg, *Work on Myth*, trans. Robert M. Wallace (Cambridge, MA, 1985), 523ff.].

68. German text in HA, 13:47; French translation in L. Lichenberger, *La Sagesse de Goethe* (Geneva, 1921), 69.

69. In HA, 1:722.

70. *Conversations with Eckermann* [Tuesday, March 11, 1828, in Goethe, *Goethes Gespräche*, ed. Biedermann, 3:497, no. 2578].

71. *Zum Shakespeares-Tag*, HA, 12:226.

72. *Poetry and Truth*, chap. 20, HA, 10:186.

73. Schopenhauer, *Prize Essay on the Freedom of the Will* [trans. C. Janaway in Arthur Schopenhauer, *The Two Fundamental Problems of Ethics*, in *The Cambridge Edition of the Works of Schopenhauer*, ed. Janaway (Cambridge, UK, 2009), 109].

74. Cf. below, p. 113.

75. Goethe's commentary on the fourth stanza of the *Urworte*, in *Poésies*, 2: 761.

76. Cf. W. S. Heckscher, "Goethe im Banne der Sinnbilder," in *Emblem und Emblematikrezeption*, ed. S. Penkert (Darmstadt, 1978), 355–80; Th. Buck, *Goethes Urworte. Orphisch*, 38.

77. W. S. Heckscher, "Goethe im Banne der Sinnbilder," 260 (O. Vaenius, *Emblemata sive Symbola*, [Brussels, 1624]).

78. *Conversations with Eckermann*, March 5, 1830 [Goethe, *Goethes Gespräche*, ed. Biedermann, 4:222, no. 2791, where the quotation occurs in a conversation with Soret, and the wording differs slightly from that quoted by Hadot].

79. Cf. E. Klessmann, *Christiane, Goethes Geliebte und Gefährtin* (Darmstadt, 1992), 46.

80. F. Gundolf, *Goethe*, vol. 2 (Paris, 1934), 252.

81. Goethe, *Oeuvres en 10 vol.*, trans. J. Porchat (Paris, 1861–63), 1:128 [Goethe, BA, *Poetische Werke*, 1:204–6].

82. Cf. Klessmann, *Christiane, Goethes Geliebte und Gefährtin*, 67; S. Damm, *Christiane und Goethe* (Frankfurt, 1998), 243.

83. Theocritus, in *Bucoliques grecs*, p. 74.

84. In *Briefe an Goethe*, HA, 1:305 [letter of April 1798].

85. Cf. above, p. 99.

86. *Faust II*, act 1, ll.5573–75.

87. In Goethe, *Poésies*, 2:657

88. Cf. the works by E. Klessmann and by S. Damm, cited above, note 82.

89. Ch. Du Bos, *Goethe*, 54.

90. Ch. Daremberg and E. Saglio, *Dictionnaire des Antiquités grecques et romains*, article "Nodus," 4:88.

91. A. Fowler, *Spenser and the Numbers of Time* (London, 1964), 161.

92. J.-P. Bayard, *Le Symbolisme du caducée* (Paris, 1987).

93. P. Hadot, "Emblèmes et symboles goethéens. Du caducée d'Hermès à la plante archétype," in *L'Art des confins. Mélanges offerts à Maurice de Gandillac* (Paris, 1985), 438–44.

94. Goethe, "Erläuterung zu dem aphoristischen Aufsatz 'Die Natur,'" HA, 13:48.

95. Ibid.

96. On Hope in Goethe, cf. J. Muller, "Bild und Sinnbild der Hoffnung in Goethes Werk," *Wissenschaftliche Zeitschrift der Friedrich-Schiller-Universität Jena* 3 (1952–54): 109–14; B. Hillebrand, "Die Hoffnung des alten Goethe," in *Abhandlungen der Klasse der Literatur, Akademie der Wissenschaften und der Literatur* (Mainz, 1983). This excellent study was of great help to me when writing the following pages.

97. Cf. above, pp. 92–93.

98. Sophocles, *Antigone*, l. 332 [Sophocles, *Antigone, The Women of Trachis, Philoctetes, Oedipus at Colonus*, ed. and trans. Hugh Lloyd-Jones (Cambridge, MA, 1994)].

168 NOTES TO PAGES 116–122

99. Seneca, *Letters to Lucilius*, 102.21 [Seneca, *Epistles*, vol. 3: *Epistles 93–124*, trans. Richard M. Gummere (Cambridge, MA, 1925)].

100. *On the Sublime*, 35.2–3, p. 50 [translation, modified, from Aristotle, Longinus, Demetrius, *Poetics. Longinus: On the Sublime. Demetrius: On Style*, trans. Stephen Halliwell, W. Hamilton Fyfe, Doreen C. Innes, W. Rhys Roberts, rev. Donald A. Russell (Cambridge, MA, 1995)].

101. Kant, *What Is Enlightenment?* [Immanuel Kant, *Toward Perpetual Peace and Other Writings on Politics, Peace, and History*, ed. Pauline Kleingeld, trans. David L. Colcasure (New Haven, 2006), 17].

102. Condorcet, *Esquisse d'un tableau historique des progrès de l'esprit humain*, ed. A. Pons (Paris, 1988), 265, 267, 295.

103. Hesiod, *Works and Days*, ll.92–106.

104. S. Noica, "La boîte de Pandore et l'ambiguïté de l'Elpis," *Platón* (Athens, 1984), 100–124.

105. Ibid., 116.

106. Cf. P. Mazon, in *Hésiode, Les Travaux et les Jours*, 72.

107. Babrius, *Mythiambi Aesopei*, ed. M. J. Luzzato and A. La Penna (Leipzig, 1986), 58–59, no. 58.

108. Theognis, *Elegiac poems*, I, l. 1135.

109. *Palatine Anthology*, 9.49 [translation, modified, in *The Greek Anthology*, vol. 3, book 9: *The Declamatory Epigrams*, trans. W. R. Paton (Cambridge, MA, 1917)].

110. See, on this subject, the excellent study by E. Cassirer, "Goethes Pandora," in *Idee und Gestalt. Goethe, Schiller, Hölderlin, Kleist* (Darmstadt, 1981), 7–32.

111. Cf. Goethe, *Pandora*, in *Théâtre complet*, 897 [HA, 5:344–55].

112. *Théâtre complet*, 905, 907 [HA, 5:342].

113. Ibid., 909 [HA, 5:344].

114. In HA, 5:693–95.

115. E. Cassirer, "Goethes Pandora," 23.

116. *Des Epimenides Erwachen*, ll.616ff., HA, 5:387.

117. HA, 5:750.

118. Cf. above, pp. 64–65.

119. Several commentators have identified Hope and poetry, for instance Ch. Du Bos, *Goethe*, 54; P. Citati, *Goethe* (Paris, 1992), 433; W. Emrich, *Die Symbolik von Faust II* (Frankfurt, 1964), 108.

120. Cf. above, p. 80.

121. Goethe, *West-East Divan*, 393 [BA, *Poetische Werke*, 3:254].

122. Th. Buck, *Goethes Urworte. Orphisch*, 60.

123. Cf. infra, p. 136.

124. Goethe, *Poésies*, 1:381 [BA, *Poetische Werke*, 1: 313–15].

125. *Conversations with Eckermann*, 269, February 4, 1829 [*Goethes Gespräche*, ed. Biedermann, 4:62, no. 2652]. See also the interview with Chancellor F. v. Müller, October 10, 1823, p. 132 [*Goethes Gespräche*, ed. Biedermann, 3:26, no. 2173], on the impossibility for a thinking being to imagine a cessation of life.

126. W. Benjamin, *Œuvres choisies* (Paris, 1959), 113, who explains this demand by the fear of death.

127. *Conversations with Eckermann*, February 25, 1824, pp. 99–100 [*Goethes Gespräche*, ed. Biedermann, 3:76–77, no. 2230].

128. *Faust II*, act 5, ll.11580–86.

Chapter 4

1. Cf. above, pp. 29 and 38.

2. Ibid., p. 37.

3. Ibid., pp. 66–67 and 75.

4. Ibid., p. 19.

5. Ibid., pp. 29 and 38.

6. Goethe, *Winckelmann*, HA, 12:98. On the possible origins of this text, cf. H. Nohle, "Wozu dient all der Aufwand von Sternen und Planeten," *Die Sammlung* 8 (1953): 166–70.

7. *Conversations with Eckermann*, 394, February 28, 1831 [468, ed. Beutler].

8. Hölderlin, *Poèmes (Gedichte)*, trans. G. Bianquis (Paris, 1943), 440–41, *Fragments*, I. See also Hölderlin, *Œuvres* (Paris, 1967), 926.

9. *Poésie et Vérité*, 315 [HA, 9:489].

10. *Conversations with Eckermann*, 241, June 15, 1828 [468, ed. Beutler].

11. I owe a great deal, in this exposition, to the pages W. Schadewaldt has devoted to the concept of reality in Goethe in his work *Goethestudien. Natur und Altertum* (Zürich, 1963), 247–49.

12. Goethe to Schiller, June 14, 1796, HA, 2:225.

13. *Conversations with Eckermann*, February 28, 1831 [468, ed. Beutler].

14. *Acts of the Apostles*, 17:28.

15. Aratus, *Phenomena*, l. 6.

16. Cf. above, pp. 29 and 38.

17. Cf. above, pp. 26–27.

18. Ibid., pp. 65–67.

19. Goethe, *Poésies*, 2:744–45 [BA, *Poetische Werke*, 2:103].

20. Cf. above, p. 106.

21. *Faust I*, Prologue, ll. 285–86.

22. Goethe, *Romans*, 67 [HA, 7:52–53].

23. Review of Sulzer, *Die schönen Künste*, HA, 12:17–18.

24. *One and All*, trans. J.-F. Angelloz, in *Les Pages immortelles de Goethe*, ed. H. Carossa (Paris, 1942), 171. See also *Poésies*, 2: 659 [BA, *Poetische Werke*, 1: 540–41].

25. *Testament*, l. 3, in *Poésies*, 2:747 [BA, *Poetische Werke*, 1:541].

26. *One and All*, after the translation by J.-F. Angelloz, 171. Cf. also *Poésies*, 2: 657 [BA, *Poetische Werke*, 1:540].

27. Goethe, *Poésies*, 2:200.

28. Ibid., 201.

29. M. Hulin, *La mystique sauvage* (Paris, 1993), 56–58.

30. *Rêveries du promeneur solitaire* (Paris, 1964), 129, seventh promenade.

31. *Blessed Longing*, in *Book of the Singer, West-Eastern Divan*, 81 [BA, 3:21].

32. On this subject, cf. W. Benjamin, "Les affinités électives de Goethe," in *Œuvres choisies* (Paris, 1959), 113.

33. Schelling, *Aphorisms on the Philosophy of Nature*, § 1, in *Œuvres métaphysiques (1805–1851)*, trans. J. Fr. Courtine and E. Martineau (Paris, 1980), 75; id., *Les Âges du monde*, trans. S. Jankélévitch (Paris, 1949), 162. Cf. P. Hadot, *Veil of Isis*, 300ff.

34. *Conversations with Falk* (June 14, 1809), in *Goethes Gespräche*, ed. Biedermann, 2: 40, no. 1185. The word "signature" is inherited from the Renaissance, particularly from Paracelsus: in its signature, each thing presents the expression both of its own qualities and of those of universal Nature.

35. *Maximen und Reflexionen*, §752, HA, 12:471.

36. *Maximen und Reflexionen*, §§16–17, HA, 12:367.

37. *Faust II*, act 1, ll.6271–74.

38. Ch. Andler, *Nietzsche. Sa vie et sa pensée*, vol. 1 (Paris, 1958), 20–32.

39. Nietzsche, *Twilight of the Idols; Forays of an Untimely Man*, §49 [KSA, 6: 152].

40. Nietzsche, *Posthumous Fragments* (early 1888–early January 1889, 14 [14]) [KSA 13:224].

41. Nietzsche, *Posthumous Fragments* (late 1886–spring 1887), 7 [38] [KSA, 13:307–8].

42. Cf. above, p. 127.

43. Cf. above, pp. 127 and 137.

44. Nietzsche, *Ecce Homo, Why I Am So Smart*, §10 [KSA, 6:297].
See also *Posthumous Fragments* (Spring–Summer 1888), 16 [32] [KSA, 13:492–93].

45. Nietzsche, *Dithyrambs of Dionysos, Glory and Eternity*, 4 [KSA, 6:405].

46. J. Le Rider, *Malwida von Meysenberg* (Paris, 2005), 377.

47. Nietzsche, *Nietzsche contra Wagner*, Epilogue § 1 [KSA, 6:426].

48. Marcus Aurelius, *Writings for himself*, 3.16.3.

49. Ibid., 6.45.1.

50. Ibid., 12.23.4.

51. Ibid., 3.2.

52. Nietzsche, *The Dawn*, §195 [KSA, 3:168]. On "spiritual exercises" in Nietzsche, cf. H. Hutter, *Shaping the Future. Nietzsche's New Regime of the Soul and Its Ascetic Practices* (Lanham, MD, 2005).

53. *West-Eastern Divan, Himet Nameh, Book of Maxims*, 152–53 [BA, *Poetische Werke*, 3:75].

54. WA, 4:49, 87.

55. Goethe, *Conversations with Chancellor Von Müller*, August 12, 1827, p. 21 [*Goethes Gespräche*, ed. Biedermann, 3:420, no. 2159,].

56. Cf. Goethe, "Mahomet," in the "Notes and Dissertations by the Author" to the *West-Eastern Divan*, 342 [BA, 3:183–87].

57. A. G. Baumgarten, *Aesthetica*, §§ 423, 429. Cf. P. Hadot, *Veil of Isis*, 213f.

58. *Poetry and Truth*, book 13, p. 372 [HA, 10:579–80].

59. Ibid., p. 374 [HA, 10:584].

60. Ibid., p. 371 [HA, 10:579], and cf. above, pp. 64–65.

61. *Wilhelm Meister's Journeyman Years* [2.7; BA, 8:237; p. 263, trans. Winston/Brown].

62. "Prolog zur Eröffnung des Berliner Theaters," in *Goethe, Werke, Briefe und Gespräche, Gedenkausgabe*, ed. E. Beutler, 2nd ed. (Zürich), 3:650–53.

63. Nietzsche, *Birth of Tragedy*, §24 [KSA, 1:152].

64. Nietzsche, *Posthumous Fragments (Fall 1885–Fall 1886)*, 2 [114] [KSA, 12:119].

65. Ibid.

66. Ibid.

67. Nietzsche, *Posthumous Fragments (Spring 1888)*, 14 [47] [KSA, 13:241].

68. Rilke, *Sonnets to Orpheus*, 1.7.

Conclusion

1. [Hadot, *Veil of Isis*, 299.]
2. [Ibid., 127.]
3. *Faust I*, l.1237.
4. *Wilhelm Meister's Journeyman Years*, 2.9 [HA, 8:263].
5. Cf. above, p. 15.
6. Montaigne, *Essais*, 3.13 (Paris, 1962), 1088 [Michel de Montaigne, *The Complete Essays*, trans. and ed. M. A. Screech (London, 2003)].
7. Cf. above, p. 129.

Bibliography

Works by Goethe

Editions of the German texts

BA (Berliner Ausgabe) = *Johann Wolfgang von Goethe*, ed. Siegfried Seidel, 22 vols. (Berlin: Aufbau, 1960–).

HA (Hamburger Ausgabe) = *Goethes Werke*, ed. E. Trunz, 14 vols. (Hamburg, 1948–69; rpt. Munich, 1981–82).

JA (Jubiläums-Ausgabe) = *Goethes Sämtliche Werke*, 40 vols., Stuttgart-Berlin, 1902.

WA (Weimarer Ausgabe) = *Goethes Werke*, ed. Sophie von Sachsen, 63 vols. (Weimar, 1887–1919).

Goethes Briefe, Hamburger Ausgabe, 4 vols., and *Briefe an Goethe*, 2 vols., ed. K.-R. Mandelkow (Hamburg, 1965–67; rpt. Munich, 1976–82).

Goethes Gespräche, ed. F. von Biedermann, 5 vols. (Leipzig, 1909–11).

Main Translations Used

Goethe, Johann Wolfgang von. *Conversations de Goethe avec Eckermann.* French trans. J. Chuzeville. Ed. C. Roëls. Paris, 1988.

——————. *Divan occidental-oriental.* French trans. and ed. H. Lichtenberger. Paris: Aubier, collection bilingue des classiques étrangers, 1940.

——————. *Entretiens avec le chancelier de Müller.* French trans. A. Béguin. Paris, 1931.

_____. *Poésie et Vérité: Souvenirs de ma vie.* French trans. P. du Colombier. Paris: Aubier, domaine allemand, 1991.

_____. *Poésies.* French trans. R. Ayrault. 2 vols. Vol. 1: *Des origines au Voyage en Italie.* Paris, 1951. Vol. 2: *Du Voyage en Italie jusqu'aux derniers poèmes.* Paris, 1982.

_____. *Romans.* French trans. B. Groethuysen, P. du Colombier, and B. Briod. Paris: Gallimard, Bibliothèque de la Pléiade, 1954. *Les Souffrances du jeune Werther; Les Affinités électives; Les Années de voyage; Les Années d'apprentissage.*

_____. *Théâtre complet.* Introduction by André Gide. French trans. G. de Nerval et al. Paris: Gallimard, Bibliothèque de la Pléiade, 1951.

_____. *Voyage en Italie,* French trans. J. Naujac. Paris: Aubier, collection bilingue des classiques étrangers, 1961.

Quotations from Nietzsche are taken from Friedrich Nietzsche, *Œuvres philosophiques complètes,* ed. G. Colli and M. Montinari, French trans. J.-C. Hémery, 14 vols. (Paris, 1967–97).

The translations of Goethe and Nietzsche have often been modified.

Unless otherwise indicated, the texts of the quotations from Ammianus Marcellinus, the *Palatine Anthology,* Apollonius of Rhodes, *Orphic Argonautica,* Aristophanes, Cicero, Diodorus Siculus, *On the Sublime,* Hesiod, *Historia Augusta,* Homer, Horace, Lucretius, Marcus Aurelius (*Writings for Himself* = *Meditations* [Book 1]), Ovid, Seneca, Sophocles, and Theognis have been taken from the volumes of the Collection des Universités de France (Les Belles Lettres). The translation has sometimes been modified.

Translations from Marcus Aurelius (books 2–12) are my [i.e., Hadot's] own.

Index